As Old as Time

Lilian Bricks

Copyright © 2024 by Lilian Bricks

All rights reserved.

No portion of this book may be reproduced in any form without written permission from the publisher or author, except as permitted by U.S. copyright law.

Contents

1. Prince Adam — 1
2. Cinderella — 6
3. Prince Adam — 12
4. Cinderella — 18
5. Beast — 24
6. Cinderella — 30
7. Cinderella — 37
8. Beast — 44
9. Cinderella — 52
10. Beast — 63
11. Cinderella - I — 70
12. Cinderella - II — 78
13. Beast / Cinderella — 88
14. "The Magical Night" — 92
15. Cinderella — 98

16.	Beast	104
17.	Cinderella - I	109
18.	Cinderella - II	114
19.	Beast	120
20.	Cinderella	123
21.	Cinderella	128
22.	"Floraison de l'amour"	133
23.	Beast	139
24.	"la nuit magique"	144
25.	Lady Tremaine	153
26.	Moment de vérité - I	161
27.	Moment de vérité - II	169
28.	Moment de vérité - III	174

Prince Adam

Prince Adam dusted off his dress coat as he admired himself in the mirror. The royal hairdresser was giving the final touches to his hair and was practically shaking while doing so. Adam chuckled at him evilly before shrugging his hands off of him and nodded his head at him.

The hairdresser took it as his cue to leave and disappeared from the room in a matter of seconds as he didn't want to upset the prince. Upsetting the prince lead to many consequences and the poor hairdresser didn't have it in him to face it; the prince was cruel they said.

Adam smirked as he powdered his nose one more time, and reapplied the lipstick so that his lips stood out the most against his powdered face and gorgeous blue eyes. The colour of his lips was selected to be scarlet red for the night as he had decided that it would shine out his seductive side more.

He grabbed the blush as he smeared it out thoroughly onto his cheeks and smiled in delight as the pink powder flushed him in his innocent façade. As he decided that he was satisfied with the makeup, he snapped his fingers and in came the servants with his racks and racks full of cashmere coats, all big and lined up in his precise favourite order.

Adam turned around in his chair and stared at the many coats he owned. He felt a need to call the royal tailor and stich him up a new one. But, he was excited for the party to start and couldn't make his guests longer; even though they would do anything to please their royal prince.

He sighed and pointed his finger at a big, bright sky blue cashmere coat with white little flowers embedded on it, the same as the ones he had in his royal gardens. The head servant, immediately took it off the hanger and held it for Adam to wear. Adam stood up from his chair and turned around. The servant helped him put on the coat and they were done just like that. In mere seconds, the servants were out of his highness's room, with little to no hustle.

He walked out of his room few minutes later with a grin on and nodded at his prime minister to notion him the start of the annual party of the mighty Village. The prince hosted a ton of parties but, the annual party meant a lot more to him as it showcased his power and wealth among the rich and the poor, gaining him more respect and most importantly fear. Fear fed him as a great deal, it boosted his ego knowing he was better than other human beings.

Adam placed his hand on the hand railing and took one step at a time as he looked over the crowd waiting for him, at the end of the staircase. He smirked in delight as they were all dressed up in their best attires; up to the royal standards. He wouldn't allow anyone into the castle. The prince would himself check if everyone present was eligible to be in the castle. There were strict rules and regulations and violating them meant either of the two things- banishment from the Village or death.

"Oh, Madame Garderobe, you look beautiful as ever." Adam spoke as he reached the end of staircase and looked at Madame Garderobe waiting for him. He bowed down for her and kissed her hand before walking her to the centre of the ballroom. He smiled at the ladies standing around him in a circle and left Madame Garderobe at the centre of the circle and walked to his throne.

He walked while acknowledging his guests and turned swiftly as he reached the throne. He sat on the throne gracefully and looked over the crowd. He raised his hands up in the air and clapped twice to indicate the beginning of the night. At his signal, the guests sprinted into the dance and musicians started playing their instruments. Madame Garderobe started singing the great galore of Prince Adam and his ancestors; as she twirled amidst the guests dancing.

"Oh, how divine is the glamour music, magic and time.

As we are blessed to be here;

with a need so anxious to shine.

What every heart prays,

that every prince, every dog has its day."

Madame Garderobe kept on singing next to her beloved Lumière, who played the piano for her. She smiled at him with adoration, and raised her voice pitch for the next verse. Prince Adam got up from his throne and walked to the centre of the ballroom. He joined the beautiful ladies in the dancing and laughed loudly as he twirled a lady in his arms.

The lady smiled at him innocently and he moved on to another one, as he got bored of her beauty. She was a beauty but, not the one he desired the most. They were all beautiful as he only chose the best ones. But, he was tired of seeing the same women with loads of makeup and their puffy gowns.

Adam walked to the centre of the ballroom, doing a twirl and danced to the tune of Madame Garderobe's music as she the pace of the dancing increased and the women around him, started going around in circles. He laughed loudly at the flirtatious women and winked at the shy ones, earning him blushing faces.

The heat in the party increased as the guests started enjoying themselves with the wine and dancing going around. Prince Adam kept on moving on from one arm to another as he danced graciously with every woman.

As, he was about to twirl another woman in his arm, there was thunder and lightning out of the blue in the spring season. The music stopped at the sudden change of climate. The guests were startled as they looked out through wall length windows and saw a dark demeanour of the wind and nature.

The temperature dropped in the ballroom and Prince Adam made his way through the crowd towards the gates, to check the hindrance. Madame Garderobe grabbed Lumière's arms as she struggled to keep sense of the happenings around her. Lumière kept his arms closed around her and tried to relax her. Mr. Cogsworth walked through the crowd and stood behind Prince Adam as he tried to find the source of problem.

The candles and lamps blew out as the winds flowed that forced the main gates open with a loud noise and some of the glass windows shattered. Prince Adam's eyes widened as he stood straight and looked out the gates to spot anyone or anything. The prince focused on the gates, but all he could see was the dark black cloud.

A minute later, the winds stopped howling and the temperature dropped even more. The ballroom's environment had become tense and full of fear and dread. The guests were terrified and Prince Adam was testing his last amounts of patient. He took a step further and the dark cloud before him cleared and he saw the outline of a person.

The person, walked into the ballroom and the guests moved further back into the halls, fearing the uneventful. The person had a black coat on them as they hunched slowly into the room. At the last moment, the mysterious person collapsed on the floor and tried to stable themselves. Adam stood in front of the person, and looked at the torn coat, he laughed out loud at the poor being.

"And, who you might be?" He asked as held his nose high in the air, full of pride. The person finally looked up and the cape around them fell down against the shoulders and revealed a rather old woman; a sick old woman. Adam scrunched his face at the wrinkled face of the old woman and scoffed at her ugliness.

"Please, help me." The old woman begged for help and Adam looked her over to find any belongings. "Do you have anything to give me in return?" He asked her laughing evilly.

The woman placed her hand in the pocket of her coat and slowly with trembling hands took out a worn rose. She held it in front of Adam and said, "This is all I have to offer."

~~~

Cinderella

Ella sat at the window looking at the beautiful flowers blooming in the garden. She smiled at their colours and closed her eyes in delight. She sighed happily as she hummed a tune and nodded her head to the music.

She sat there with her hands placed in her lap and her long legs spread out in front of her. Her brunette hair swept sideways as the winds blew through the window. The melanin brown of her skin glowed as she basked in the rays of sunshine. Her mood was always happy when the weather was warm and sunny. She hated the cold with a passion as it would remind her of the dark demeanor and sadness.

At the sound of chirpings, she opened her eyes and laughed loudly as she saw the little bird trying to get into her room through the grills of her window. She placed her palm upside down and the little bird jumped onto her palm. She kissed his head lightly and the bird flapped its wings in response.

She held him in front of her and said, "Hey there, little guy. How have you been?" the bird just chirped in response to her question and she giggled, "Aren't you a cute little lad?" The bird jumped in his place and flapped his wings fast as his answer.

"Why don't you have some food, huh?" She said as she placed him back on the edge of the window and stood up to the bring him some raw rice she kept in her room, to feed birds. She grabbed some in her fist and then placed it slowly in front of the bird, careful not to spill any on the ground. "There you go, little guy." She said as she sat in front of him and saw as he picked one by one with his beak and swallowed. She patted his head softly and giggled at his attempt to fit more than one bits in his beak simultaneously.

Ella looked out the window to find her stepmother Tremaine and her stepsisters Anastasia and Drizella step down from the carriage. Even though her stepmother wasn't much of a mother towards her and her stepsisters but, Ella knew that her stepmother dotted on her sisters and nurtured them with love and care.

Looking at her stepmother, Ella remembered the fond memories of her own mother. Her mother had long wavy dark brunette hair just like her and her skin was the same colour. Ella knew that her mother was the most beautiful woman her father had seen and he loved her with all his heart. Her father was the most successful nobleman in the Village but, he would say, "I'm just a beggar in front of your mother, asking her to shower me with love and care as she is a divine human being."

Ella knew that her mother was the sweetest person in Village and everyone adored her for her beauty and kind nature. Not a single person who came asking for help at her home, would go unattended her mother used to say. A smile spread on Ella's face as she remembered her father twirling her and her mother up in the air whenever he would return from his business trips. He would shower them with kisses and gifts to make up for the time he would be away from them.

The three of them would play in the open grounds and the backyard whenever they would be together and laugh and smile. Ella's memories were all filled with love, laugh and gifts as much as she could remember.

Only one of them was bitter and it was of the time when she was fourteen. It was the year her mother had suddenly taken a catch of illness and it was the year when the distraught had been brought upon her family. Ella considered that year to be cursed. Her mother had been fine but, one day she fell unconscious in her room and the doctors had to be called in as she didn't wake up for a long period of time. Her father was by her bedside till she opened her eyes, and breathed normal again. Ella was scared and frightened that day as she was playing out in the open when the havoc started. The maids and servants were running everywhere to find medicines and whatnot.

Ella wasn't allowed to enter her parent's bedroom for her safety. Even though being clueless at her age, she had the idea that something bad had happened to her mother. Ella sat in room frightened and praying for her mother's health while clenching her favourite doll in her arms. Tears were running down her face, when the maids came in to check on her and feed her dinner. She refused to eat alone and threw a tantrum as she wanted to hear the well-being of her mother. But, none of the servants gave her an answer. She ran back to her room from the dining room and kept on crying. Later on, her father came in with the plate of food and he had fed her while caressing her and calming her down.

She asked her father out of curiosity and concern, "Papa, is Mama going to be alright?" The question threw him off the guard as he had been focussed on feeding her. With trembling hands, he had replied, "Yes, my darling. She is alright. You needn't worry. Let's finish eating this and going to bed, shall we, my love?" He had asked her with a weak smile.

"Can I see Mama? I really want to see her face, Papa." Ella had replied with a frown and her father's eyes widened, "You see, my love, your Mama is tired and she has already gone to bed. You should too." He held her chin his hand as he told her, "You know Mama gets angry when you stay past bedtime, right?" She nodded at him in horror as she knew Mama would get angry if she broke any of the rules.

Her father had smiled at her response and after tucking her in bed, he had left after placing a kiss on her forehead. Ella slept peacefully that night as her father had fed her himself and she knew that her mother's health was good but, when she woke up next morning, she felt a change in the atmosphere. The wind was chilly and the sun wasn't shining brightly nor were the animals out in the open. The only sound of the rustling of the leaves amongst themselves was heard and Ella walked over her bedroom door and opened it slowly. There was no one in the corridor so, with small steps she reached the living room and saw the servants all lined up looking sad and some were crying.

When no one paid attention to her presence she had muttered a small, "Hello." And it was enough for them to wipe out their tears and her father was called in the living room.

When her father walked her, Ella was sat on one of the sofa chairs and she stood up and ran towards her father to hug him, "Papa!" She exclaimed as she clung on to his legs. Her father took her hands in his and bent down to her height. "Ella, my love." He spoke, "You get to see your Mama." This made a smile spread across her face but, it dropped when he continued on further, "Ella, your Mama is sick and these are her last moments. You need to be brave my child." He kissed her forehead as he hugged her tightly and a single tear rolled on to his cheeks.

Ella had never seen her father cry, so this was a grand moment for her, as she swept the rolling tear with thumb and whispered, "Yes, Papa. I'll be brave." Her father looked at her while crying and asked, "You understand?" She nodded at him in response and he stood up. He took her hand in his and walked her over to their bedroom. He opened the door and there her mother sat on the chair, covered in blankets. She looked beautiful as she always did but, as Ella walked into the room, Ella recognised the dullness of her mother's skin and the hollowness in her cheeks. There were bags under her eyes and when she heard Ella walk in, she turned towards her slowly, "Ella, my child." She said with a fragile voice and took her hands in hers when Ella reached her chair.

Her mother looked tired and lifeless as Ella stared at her. Her mother caressed her hands as she spoke, "Ella, my love. You need to learn the greatest secret of living a blissful life." Ella nodded at her to continue, "You need to always be kind and have courage, Ella." Ella smiled at her through her tears and placed a kiss on her mother's forehead. Her mother smiled at her weakly and said "You should always treat people with kindness, Ella." These were her mother's last words before her eyes suddenly closed and her hand fell from Ella's grip.

Ella's eyes widened at this and she stood there shocked, just as her father dragged her out of the room. She didn't realise that she had started screaming and scratching and kicking around to not to get out of her mother's bedroom. She wanted to be with her till her last moments. The doctors had rushed in along with maids and nurses to help them out.

Ella had stopped screaming when the doctors finally emerged out of the room, she looked at them hopefully but her hope died when they shook her head at her father. Even fourteen-year-old Ella knew what the look meant and after that she had gone into fits of crying for hours. Her father had suffered a huge heart break but, he was coping better than her. When one of the nights, she remembered her mother's words- "Have courage and be kind." Ella had stopped crying and she walked into her father's room to hug him and tell him, "It's going to be okay, Papa. We'll be okay."

Just like that the father and daughter duo had slowly learnt how to live without her mother and there were times when they both missed her, but they somehow managed. After a year or so, her father had started going back on business trips, leaving Ella with the maids and servants back. She would always ask him to get her a memorable gift from his trips and he never forgot.

A year ago, he had said to her when he returned from one of his trips, "My dear Ella, I think it's time for me to move on." He had hesitated first but when Ella placed her hands on his trembling hands, he had continued, "I think it's in my best interest to meet someone." Ella had smiled at him and said, "I think so, too Papa. You should be happy too." Her father had smiled at her and said, "I mean your Mama would want me to be happy, right?" and she had replied, "Yes, Papa!"

After a short while her stepmother Tremaine and her father had gotten married and she had moved in with them, along with her stepdaughters. Ella was trying to recall the next moment when the door to her room swung open and there stood her Papa still in his business attire, looking happy and energetic, "Ella, my love!" He exclaimed as soon as he saw his beautiful teenager daughter.

Ella's smiled widened at his sight as he had gone for over more than three months and she had missed him terribly. "I missed you, Papa." She said as she ran over to him and hugged him tightly.

"I missed you too, my child." Her father said, eyes full of tears and adoration.

~~~

Prince Adam

Adam laughed at her as he saw the small rose she held in her fragile hands, "What kind of joke is this?" He asked her, "Is this all you have?" The old woman rose her head a little to look at him, and nodded her head at his question.

Prince Adam scoffed at her response and shook his head. He looked at her and made a double check. She had a huge black, torn cloak over her old torn clothes. Her hair was all over the place and smelt bad. Adam scrunched up his nose at her body odour.

"Why should I help you?" The prince asked the old woman with an evil laugh and smirked. The old woman shuddered at him and spread her hands in front of him begging for him to help her, "Please, please help me. Help me!"

"I won't be getting any benefit from saving an old, ugly woman like yours. No one wants an ugly woman in their house, do they?" Adam bent down at her level and asked her with a laugh, shaking his head at her.

"Do they?" He stood up abruptly as he turned around and asked the guests loudly. "Answer me!" He shouted at them and they immediately nodded their head at him as an answer.

Lumière and Madame Garderobe were scarred at their Prince's behaviour as they knew how much he despised ugly and poor people. Let alone this woman had interrupted his highness's annual party. They knew how quickly the things would get out of hands. The environment was silent and the temperature had dropped considerably low.

The Prince walked in a circle as he placed a finger on his chin, his stance in a thinking demeanour. He circled around her and looked at his guests, "What shall we do about her? Tell me, my people." He asked them as he looked at the old woman with disgust.

Mrs. Potts hugged Chip in her arms, as Chip was terrified of the thunder and lightning. She looked at Adam with concern in her eyes, as he had the habit of overdoing things. She looked at Lumière and nodded at him to do something but, Lumière was helpless as no one could ever his Highness from doing what he wanted. Mr. Cogsworth stepped forward upon seeing the distress among the guests. He spoke softly, "Your Highness, I think you should just let her in, in the servant's cottage. She just needs a place for the night." But, before he could speak further on, Adam snapped his fingers and shook his head, "No, no Cogsworth. We can't let her off so easily." He smirked at him sideways, "After all, she had the audacity to stop my annual party."

Madame Garderobe gasped at this, as she knew that this meant the inhumane insult. She shook her head at Lumière and looked at him for help. Lumière was about to walk over to Prince Adam when, Adam bent down in front of the old woman and extended his hand for her.

The time stopped for everyone as it was the first time, Prince Adam had held his hand out to help someone as, he was arrogant and unkind. It was pin drop silence in the ballroom as everyone waited for the old woman to place her hand in his. The old woman smiled at him, and slowly placed her fragile palm in his hand.

Adam helped her stand slowly, waiting for her to take her time. As she finally stood up, Adam bowed down in front of her in regards. The woman gave him a weak smile and turned around as he walked her.

"Would you mind giving me that rose, my lady?" Adam asked her softly. She nodded at him slowly and placed her other hand inside her cloak to retrieve the rose. Adam smiled widely at her as he took the rose from her hands. He held in his other hand, while the other hand escorted the old woman.

They walked slowly towards the door and as they reached the main gate, Adam turned towards her and said, "My lady, this is where you will be living."

The old woman in confusion looked around the surroundings, only to find the chilling atmosphere of the night and the garden outside the castle. She turned towards Adam to find him smirking, "Where, my prince?" she asked him.

"Outside." He pointed, "Where you belong. There is no place for a woman like you in my castle." He shouted as he pushed her out of his castle and looked at the rose she gave him. The woman fell hard against the cold floor and tried to contain herself. She looked horrified as she saw the evil persona of Adam reflect in his eyes.

Adam scoffed as he spoke, "You thought, you would give me a rose and I would let you in my castle for a shelter?" He threw the rose at her and said, "This is my castle, not an orphanage to let anyone in. Only those who are honoured enough can place a foot here with my permission."

He turned around and the woman struggled to get to her feet, as she was about to speak again, Adam closed the gates on her face. He looked at the guests, who seemed horrified to say the least. He shook his head, "Why the delay? Let's continue the party without any disturbance or nuisance." The guests scrambled and quickly took their positions, waiting for the music to start.

Just as he walked towards the centre of the room, there was a bright glow through the main gates, everyone grew silent. Adam stopped in tracks and turned sideways to see the light. He looked at the gates and saw the intensity of the light increasing ten folds. The glow reflected in his eyes, as he saw the glass of the gates shatter on the ground in pieces. The gates swung open and Adam bent down to protect himself from the shattered glass pieces.

He squinted his eyes, to look through the light. He walked towards the gates, only to shut his eyes from the glow. He saw the cloak of the old woman lying on the ground and he looked up to see a beautiful Enchantress in the air. He looked at her with adoration.

Her beauty was unspeakable as her skin was as porcelain as marble and her lips were more red than the rose. The blush in her cheeks resembled the pinkness of the sunset and her hair was as gold as the desert sand. The aura around her grew as she rose up slowly in the air.

Adam's eyes widened as he stared at the Enchantress. He was smitten at her beauty and stood in his place in awe. The Enchantress looked at the crowd and smirked at Adam. "You rejected me because I was ugly. Now, look at me but, you can't have me." Adam gasped at this and stepped back in shock.

"You have no sense of mannerisms and kindness." She spoke with disgust. "You need to learn how to respect, love and be kind." She spoke with so much angst that someone got scarred and screamed loudly. The crowd starting running haywire as they hadn't ever seen a magical Enchantress. The crowd ran towards the gates to run away from the wrath of the Enchantress.

Adam was stuck on his spot as he looked at the Enchantress. Lumière and Madame Garderobe held each other tightly as they feared for their lives as the Enchantress's aura grew warmer around them. Mrs. Potts searched for Chip in the crowd and called out his name to find him. Adam was enchanted and the Enchantress's aura grew in anger.

"I offered you a rose, more powerful and beautiful than everything in the world and you rejected it. You have to earn the right to live as a human again." She looked at him with hatred. It was forbidden for the Enchantress to feel anything other than love and this terrified Mr. Cogsworth.

"You shall be punished for this." The Enchantress cursed out loud. "You shall live as the ugliest, most horrifying and hideous creature. You shall live a life crueller than an animal." She cast her wand at him and a light struck out from it and hit Adam straight in the chest.

Adam fell back a step due to the force and down on his knees. He looked at his hands and his widened as he realized that fur was growing all over his body rapidly.

The Enchantress threw the rose at his feet and said, "This is your last hope to become human again. You monster." And with a snap of fingers she disappeared from the castle.

Adam struggled to walk as his legs changed from human's to animalistic form. He gripped the chair as he stumbled over his own legs. The guests had vacated the ballroom and now it was just Mr. Cogsworth, Madame Garderobe, Lumière, Mrs. Potts, Chips- the loyal servants. They saw as their Prince stumbled around the room to get a touch of reality but, he failed as his arrogance had bought him this fate.

Mrs. Potts closed Chip's eyes as their beloved Prince turned into a Beast and the fur on his body grew. His hands turned into claws and he enlarged in size. He threw around the chairs and table to find a mirror as he couldn't believe his own eyes.

The servants slowly changed into objects and were terrified as Lumière turned into a candle stand, Madame Garderobe into a wardrobe, Mr. Cogsworth into a clock, Mrs. Potts into a Tea Pot, Chip into a tea cup. Their prince tore his clothes slowly as he felt the pain of bones cracking and reshaping.

All the candles of the castle blew out as the winds flowed and the temperature dropped abruptly in the room and as Madame Garderobe looked out the windows she saw that the gates of the castle were rotten and the garden had dried out. The whole Village seemed miles apart from the castle and they were trapped in the castle.

Everyone gasped as they heard the shattering of the mirror glass and saw that the prince had finally seen his new form and looked into the mirror. The mirror was half broken and he could only see his half face but, that was enough for him to lose the last bit of patience as he threw the mirror away in disgust.

He looked at the rose lying on the floor and picked it slowly with fragile hands as it was his last hope of becoming human again. He clenched it in his hands and he's gaze was longing as he ran off with it towards his quarters.

It was the look of vulnerability his servants would see in a long time.

~~~

Cinderella

Ella smiled at her father as she placed the cup of tea on the table. Her stepmother, Lady Tremaine sat next to her father on the sofa and read the newspaper.

"There you go, Papa." Ella said as she sat next to him. Her father was in the middle of signing another business deal and he smiled at her as he put the papers down. He stretched his hands and twirled his neck before picking up the tea cup from the table. He took a sip and sighed in delight as the tea helped him relax from the working stress.

The room felt afresh due to the recent sprinkling of the rose water, Ella had just done. Ella fidgeted in her seat as she slowly turned towards her father and asked, "How is it, Papa?" Ella saw her stepmother roll her eyes in her peripheral vision, but, she ignored her as she focused on her father.

"Ahh, darling." Her father began and then released a pleasing sigh, "It's lovely as ever and the taste is sweet as you are. Thank you for this, my love." He said as he turned around in his place to face her and placed a hand on her head to pat her lovingly.

Her stepmother cleared her throat breaking the lovely moment between the father-daughter duo, and began, "Ella, darling. Why don't you bring your father the cookies you baked?" She said slightly nodding her head towards Ella.

Upon hearing this, Ella jumped to her feet as she almost forgot about those cookies, "Yes, Papa." She said as she walked towards the kitchens, "I'll be back in a second." Her father smiled at her and she exited through the doors. As she left the room, she could see her stepmother talking to her father in hushed tones.

Ella's face scrunched in confusion but, nonetheless she continued walking towards the kitchens. As she walked towards her kitchen, she heard some soft mumbling and thudding coming from the staircase leading to her room, she walked in the direction only to find Jaq and Gus fighting each other over a piece of cheese.

Ella laughed lightly at their little fight and this seemed to break them apart, they both look at Ella in horror as they realized they had been found. Ella tried to excel a stern look without doubling over with laughter and it worked but, then she lost her control and laughed loudly. Jaq and Gus, scratched their head nervously and Ella bent down to pat their heads, she placed her palm on the ground for them to climb up and they do it without hesitation.

She turned towards the kitchen and began, "What have I told you both?" She asks them with a stern gaze and they shy away from her question, "You know better than to fight over food." She reached the kitchens while scolding them and as she entered, a loud thud sounds from the cabinet and Ella stopped in her tracks.

Jaq and Gus both turn their heads to look for the source of sound and Ella walked faster further into the kitchen. As she rounded the kitchen island, she saw Anastasia and Drizella bent down on the ground haphazardly trying to gather the cookie crumb off the kitchen floor. Their dresses are covered in cookie batter and their hair is sticking out in every direction as they had been fighting.

They are still unaware of Ella's presence and Ella smiled amusingly at the mice, they smirk back at her. Ella folded her hands as she waited for them to finish up clearing the evidence.

"What are you doing, idiot?" Anastasia mumbled to Drizella, "We weren't supposed to finish it all off!" She bangs Drizella's head against the drawers and Drizella winces at the pain and smacks Anastasia's hands off her head.

"It's all your fault." Drizella spoke with annoyance in her tone, "Your pretty head doesn't know that its dumb. You just couldn't stop eating it." She exclaimed as she gathered the crumb together to pick them up.

"What was I supposed to do, ugly head?" Anastasia replied with a sigh and she looked at the cookie crumb with adoration, "They are just so good." She stopped collecting them and just looked at them, "Why did she have to make them so tasty?" She cried hysterically.

Ella looked at them and placed her palm on her mouth from laughing out loud. Amusement reflected in her eyes and Jaq and Gus looked at her in adoration as she hadn't looked so happy in a long time. But, sadly the moment didn't last long as her father and stepmother walked into the kitchen upon hearing the commotion and her father asked, "What is going on here?" As he stood next to Ella. Her stepmother scrunched up her face in disgust as she saw her daughters looking so ungraceful and full of dirt.

Her stepsisters, stood up abruptly at the voices and tried to straighten their appearances as much as possible but, failed to do so. Her stepmother looked at them and spoke with disgust, "What are you two dimwit doing? Quickly change your clothes and wash your faces." Ella stood there giggling as they tried to rush out of the kitchen with utmost grace but, with their appearances it wasn't helping them at all. Her father left them alone with a small laugh, and Tremaine turned towards Ella with a scowl on her face, "Why are you standing there laughing, Ella? Clean up the mess your sisters made." She said with a stern voice and Ella scrambled to the floor with the cloth as she didn't want her stepmother to get angry. Jaq and Gus rushed to the corner as they were terrified of Tremaine, her posture and aura was quite the extreme dark, full of angst.

Ella got on her knees and started scrubbing the wet patches off the floor. She didn't dare look her stepmother in the eyes, her heart was racing fast and she was terrified. She could hear her stepsisters giggling in the background but she didn't dare lift her eyes off the floor.

Just as she finished scrubbing the floor, she heard her stepmother say, "This is what you should do, Ella." Ella looked up and found her smirking down on her. Her mother was about to say more when her father walked back into the kitchen, "What are you saying to her, Tremaine?" Her father asked her to check if he had heard her correctly. Her stepmother's persona changed upon hearing her father's voice and she smiled at Ella before continuing, "All I was saying that Ella should continue making her delicious cookies." Her father seemed pleased at the answer and nodded at her, "That's true, darling." He smiled at Ella and looked at Tremaine, "Shall we continue with the work, my lady?"

Tremaine nodded at him quickly and turned to leave but, not before she glanced back at Ella and gave her a dirty look. Ella, the innocent child seemed lost with her stepmother's behaviour.

~~~

Ella smiled slightly as she hummed a song as she walked along the corridor after dinner that night. A book in her hand, she turned the page and with the little bounce in her feet, she walked towards the living room.

Her family had just finished dinner and she had helped the maids with the cleaning of the dishes. She loved doing chores as they kept her busy during her free time and the maids could also use a helping hand. Her mother had taught her to be helpful to every living being.

She could hear the faint sounds of her stepsisters fighting over a dress from upstairs and she smiled at their goofiness. She was glad to have them as she had been a single child and even though they were silly at times, they were still her siblings.

In her peripheral vision, she saw Jaq and Gus enter the room. She tried to fake ignore them and pretend to be engrossed in her book but, when they tugged on her dress, she couldn't resist them.

She closed her book with her bookmark in place and bent down, "And what are you both up to?" She asked them while patting their heads, but they didn't reply as they tugged on her dress and ran out of the living room. Ella took the indication as to follow us and walked in the same direction as them.

She walked out of the living room and out through the main gate, she followed them as they walked around the house and into the backyard. Her face was determined to find out what they were up to and she increased her speed as curiosity filled her mind.

A moment later they stopped and Ella ran towards them. She looked around but, couldn't find anything out of the ordinary. But, she suddenly heard voices and she looked up to find herself beneath her father's bedroom window. The mice nodded their head at her and left her alone.

She tried to focus on the voices and stilled not to make her presence noticeable. She could decipher her father's and her stepmother's voice now and she strained her ears to get a hold of their talk.

"Why don't you understand, Tremaine?" Her father reasoned out loud and she heard her stepmother sigh.

"What do you want me to understand, Baron? That you are going broke?" She heard her stepmother ask and this made Ella gasp out loud as she had never thought that they were running out of money or that her father's business was running on the low.

"Yes, is it so hard to understand?" Her father asked her in return and said, "Would it be so bad if you held your party next week? There is a lot of money spent on these parties, you know." He said as he sighed. Ella's heart broke at the sound of her father's pleading voice.

"You didn't have to marry me if you couldn't afford to keep up with my expenses." Her stepmother uttered with disgust in her tone and Ella clenched her skirt in her hands tight to control her anger.

"I can provide you with money." Her father pleaded, "Just give me a week's time and everything will be fine." She heard her father give up.

"You better or else I'll leave." Ella heard her stepmother spit out in arrogance and her heart burned knowing that her father was in stress. Ella sat on the ground and wept as she knew that her father would leave soon.

~~~

Beast

The castle was silent as the night was dark and frightening. The atmosphere resembled the deadly cursed bestowed upon the servants and the beloved prince. The cold seemed to increase as the days went by and the living beings became less humane per say. The connection to the outer world was cut off and no one knew what was going on every day for past five years.

Lumière sat on the window sill looking out and watching as the snow fell continuously; piling throughout the garden and the trees, making them isolated more and more.

Lumière sighed as he wondered when he would be able to become human again and kiss his lover, the Featherduster. He missed his days as the prince's apprentice, riding through the village delivering his announcements. The wind blew in through the gap between the window sills and blew off the candle on top his head. He lit it up again using his left hand's candle. He placed his right arm on his knees as he rested, looking all sad and gloomy. Even though he had become a candle stand after the Enchantress's curse, he felt lucky being a special, vintage candle.

"Why do you look so sad, my darling?" He heard Featherduster speak from beside him and he turned to look at her.

"It's just a gloomy day, isn't darling?" He said as he jumped down from the window sill and walked over to where she stood. He took her in his arms, caressing her shoulders lightly and he smiled at her. "It indeed is." She replied as she rested her head against his shoulders.

Lumière placed his left hand against the small curve of her waist and took her right hand in his and started moving around the floor. It was quite frightening how they always found comfort in each other's arms, even though the possibility of them becoming human again decreased as the days went by.

Featherduster had always been a beautiful woman and she brought brightness wherever she went, her personality was charming to say the least. She had turned into a beautiful pigeon shaped featherduster. It suited her perfectly, Lumière used to say. Although, the whiteness of her duster form contrasted against her skin colour; it was an amazing golden skin tone. She didn't mind it though. She knew that Lumière would love her no matter her skin colour.

Their small dance was broken midway as they heard a cough from the doors. Lumière's senses were quick and he walked towards the noise. He slowly stood against the door and leaned down a little bit to see the cause of the sound. There was a huge shadow across the wall as the person walked upwards and Lumière was afraid as no person had walked through the castle since the last five years. Lumière rubbed his hands together ready to burn the person as his defence. But, there was a cough from the person and the shadow seemed to grow as they walked up the stairs. Lumière's heartbeat fastened and he feared for his life.

Lumière closed his eyes, ready for the attack but, as soon as he opened his eyes and swung his hands at the person, he heard a loud scream, "Lumière, what are you doing?" The person spoke and Lumière blinked to focus on the person. It was after all Mr. Cogsworth- "The Clock" trying to fend off the heat from the candle burns.

Lumière heaved out a huge sigh and sat down on the ground, clenching his head in hands and trying to slow down his breathing. Mr. Cogsworth shook his shoulder but, Lumière didn't reply. A second later he mustered all his strength and stood up, Mr. Cogsworth looked at him questionably and Lumière screamed at him, "Why were you walking up the stairs like that?" This startled Mr. Cogsworth and he took a step back to avoid his lashing. He struggled to speak as he shrugged, "I...I... I mean I was just tired and I was walking up really slow. One step at a time." He looked at him, innocently and Lumière couldn't help but, lower his temper.

"Then, why on earth was your shadow so huge?" Lumière reasoned out. Mr.Cogsworth looked around the staircase and shrugged as he didn't had any answer, "It must be the candles along the stairwell."

Lumière let his shoulders fall and he looked down, trying not to lash out on Mr. Cogsworth for a simple reason. Just as Mr. Cogsworth kept a hand on Lumière's shoulder and was about to lead him inside the room, they heard a loud bang. Their eyes widened as they looked at each other and knew who started the commotion.

The three of them rushed towards the east wing of the castle as fast as they could, as they reached the stairwells leading towards their Master's room, Chip the boy who had turned into a tea cup was running downstairs. He stopped as he saw them and motioned towards the room while saying, "He's mad! He's furious."

Lumière and Mr. Cogsworth looked at each other with terror in their eyes and skipped two staircases at a time, as they rushed to see what troubled their master. Chip jumped as he made his way over the kitchens. As they neared his room, they heard another loud bang and the door to his room was halfway open. They could see his shadow against the wall and from the way his body was shaking with anger, they knew it wasn't an easy night for him.

They heard Mrs. Potts- "The Tea Pot" trying to calm his anger by speaking to him a soft voice, "Darling, why don't you calm down a little bit?" His reply was that of a groan and shattering of glass. Lumière shivered at the noise and slowly opened the door to his bedroom.

His eyes widened as he took in the mess, his Master had made and his eyes settled on Mrs. Potts sitting on the table. She shook her head at me and asked him to take over. The Beast realized that Lumière was in the room and he turned towards him in anger. He walked towards him in an angry stance, while his feet stomped loudly against the floor and Lumière's heartbeat increased rapidly. His feet fell back as he tried to adjust to his Master's incredible demeanour.

His Master was affected the most, as other servants were turned into mere objects, he had been turned into a wild animal for being disrespectful and unkind. His once sweet, handsome face had now turned into one of the ugliest and scariest face, his ears had grown out like the wolves, his hands had turned into claws and his leg's structure had become similar to the wolves. His body was covered in brown fur and he had horns on his head, dark like the animals. They made him look scarier than he already did. The voice change of his didn't help the cause, as it had deepened, making them more vulnerable to his lashings.

He had changed into his worst nightmares and become one of the most hideous beast to live.

The one person who wasn't scared as the rest of the members were in the castle was Mrs. Potts. She treated him like her own child and was the sweetest to him. He didn't purposefully lash out on her but, sometimes it became too much for him to handle and today was one of those days.

"Lumière, where is the food?" The beast asked him bending down, so he was the same eye level as his, and stared deeply into his eyes.

Lumière gulped before he spoke, "It's ready to be served in the dining room, Master." He looked down as he finished the sentence and waited for another lashing but, didn't receive one as his Master threw the cupboard against the floor and Mrs. Potts gasped loudly at his actions. Before, Lumière could figure what was going on, his Master had left the room through the window yelling out, "Leave it."

Mrs. Potts sighed loudly as she knew that Master would soon come to his senses and would apologise to them for his behaviour. But, right now he needed to be left alone. Lumière sighed and looked out the window, his Master had gone out through and his heart sank with dreadfulness.

~~~

Mrs. Potts couldn't stop clutching Chip to her chest as she kissed him repeatedly for not being in the same room as Master, since Chip had the tendency to say foolish things at the wrong as he was just a boy.

Lumière and Mr. Cogsworth paced the kitchen as all the other servant members were gathered around them; trying to figure out a plan to help their Master.

Featherduster sighed heavily from her position as she spoke, "We have to help him. The time is passing by too quickly and as another petal falls, we are turning less humane."

Lumière looked up at her and said, "I know, my darling. There must be a way to help him somehow." He clucked his tongue and continued pacing around the room, holding his hands behind his back and head bent down.

Mr. Cogsworth coughed out loudly and it was real for a second but, then it was a clear indication that he wanted to say something, Lumière looked at him, nodding him to continue. Mr. Cogsworth cleared his throat before he began, "We need true love to break the curse." Everyone shook their head at this and grumbled, and some smacked their foreheads as this was the most important thing about the curse.

"Where will we find true love?" Mr. Cogsworth grumbled out and sat on the floor. "I mean, there is no one here other than us and clearly nothing has happened." He huffed out.

Mrs. Potts rolled her eyes at this and said, "Love takes time. His time will come surely."

"But, how long, Mama?" Chip asked as he bounced in his place.

"Not long, my child." Mrs. Potts replied and the crowd sighed loudly.

In this moment an idea struck in Lumière's mind and he stopped pacing. He turned towards Featherduster and said, "I think, I have an idea to break the curse." He smiled as he walked out of the room with determination.

~~~

Cinderella

Ella didn't sleep that night as she turned and twisted around in her bed, waiting for the sleep to get her but, alas she failed. Her thoughts wandered to the days when her mother was alive. They were so beautiful, happy and full of life days. Her father was the happiest she had seen him. The smile never left his face and his business's venture and earnings were good too. But, after her mother's untimely death, Ella found her father more engrossed in his business and on more trips across the country; for longer period of time. His days were longer and sleep had become almost non-existent for him.

But, after he had met Lady Tremaine, his worries had somehow lessened and he was happy in her presence; something Ella had observed throughout these months.

Lady Tremaine carried the grief on herself pretty well but, her sadness could never be reflected when she would be throwing one of her parties. She was famous amongst the Villagers for her lavish parties. It cost them a lot of money as Lady Tremaine could never be satisfied with cheap alcohol but, her father looked happy in the parties. That was the only thing that mattered to Ella, she signed as she thought about this over and over.

Ella turned in her bed once again, and now she faced the windows. The breeze of the night flowed through them and the curtains followed their movements. It was like the will of the curtains depended wholly on the wind. Her eyes traced the movements and suddenly she saw her father in place of the curtains and Lady Tremaine as the wind. Her father following her for the happiness he seeked after the love, he had once lost. Lady Tremaine unaware of the weight of happiness that rested on her, did as her heart desired.

Ella closed her eyes, not wanting to face the reality just yet. She didn't want to know that her father was not the man she once knew. She shook her head slightly to get rid of the image and waited for a moment to let the thought dissolve. She slowly opened her eyes, and sighed in relief when she saw only the curtains moving.

A man she once knew or not, he was still her father and she loved him more than anything in the world. She was going to support him no matter what, no matter what decisions he makes, she decided releasing a breath she didn't knew she was holding and closed her eyes. She fell asleep the next second, with a decision made.

~~~

Ella woke up the next morning, determined to somehow help out her father with his problems. She straightened her dress and tightened her pony as she looked into the mirror. She wore her lucky blue dress, as she believed it was magical, the one which her mother had given her as a birthday present.

She huffed out a breath, as looked out the window. It was bright and sunny outside, just as her heart desired and she knew that the day was going to end well. Ella strode out of her room and made her way downstairs, a bounce in her steps, felling with excitement.

Ella walked towards the kitchens, ready to whip out a healthy breakfast for her father, to help him with the day's work. After all, breakfast is the most important meal of the day, her mother used to say. She smiled as she poured out the floor in a bowl, along with the other ingredients. The maids gave her own space, as they could see her focus was somewhere else. She smiled at them, and continued whisking her breakfast.

She flipped the pancakes around and readied the tea. Ella cut up some fruits to go alongside the breakfast. She prepared all the favourites of her father's. She knew he would be happy after eating them. Her apron was dusted off with the flour remainder and her hair was all over the place.

She tucked her hair behind her ear with a dusted hand and swept the sweat off her cheeks with her shoulder. After an hour, she was done with the breakfast. She gattered everything on her tray and placed in on the trolley. She smiled as she glanced all over the tray, trying not to miss anything. She wiped her hands on the hand towels and took off the apron, placing it on the hanger.

Ella huffed out a breath before clenching the trolley's handle in her hands. She walked towards her father's study, where she knew he would be working. But, just as she reached the doors, her heart sank with a sudden dread and she felt nervous. She shook her head to get rid of the feelings, but was successful only a little. Nonetheless, she knocked on the door slowly, and walked in a second later when she heard her father yell, "Come in!" in a rushed tone.

Ella smiled nervously as she walked in looking down, trying not to spill anything down. But, as soon as she lifted her head to look at him, all the dread filled her heart again. She stopped moving the trolley and let her hands fall down. She stood frozen for a moment, as she saw her father moving hurriedly around his study. He rushed from one corner to another, collecting documents and necessary equipments. Ella observed the equipments and knew one thing for sure.

She heard her father stop in his tracks as he realised that she was in the room to, and turned towards her, "Ella, darling. Why are you just standing there?" He continued moving in different directions frantically.

Ella didn't reply as she tried making sense of everything, everything that was going on and everything that wasn't reality. He walked towards her and her widened as she was aware of his movements, but sighed lightly when he walked towards the drawer right next to her. He began as he shuffled through the drawers, "I was going to drop by your room, right after I was done with this." He said as he picked up whatever he was trying to find and walked back to his desk. He continued further on, "You see, Ella. I'm-"

But, Ella beat him to it, as she finished the sentence for him, "You are going back on the trip."

He turned around abruptly as he didn't expect her to know this already, "Yes. But, how did you know?" He asked her, wanting to know where she had heard it.

"I just assumed, Papa." Ella shrugged at him, trying to look nonchalant, also trying not to feel guilty about lying. She was sure her mother would be scolding her from wherever she was.

Her father walked towards her and stood in front of her. "I'm sorry, Ella." He said as he held her by her shoulders in a soft grip.

Ella looked down sadly, before saying, "But, you just returned from a trip. Why are you leaving so soon?" She asked him, staring at him longingly. She knew she would break down soon enough, but she controlled her emotions as she didn't want her father to feel guilty before leaving on his trip.

"It's for work, my child." Her father spoke as he looked disheartened to see his daughter sad. "I have to go, Ella. Do you understand?" He questioned her with a small nod and she replied with a nod.

"So," he began as he moved behind his desk, "What do you want me to bring you back from the trip?" He asked her. "Your sisters. I mean, your stepsisters have asked for parasols and lace. What will you have?" He smiled at her, which caused Ella to smile back.

Ella took a moment to think before she answered, she sat down on one of the chairs placed in front of her and leaned down as she spoke, "Bring me the first rose, you see on your journey." She smiled as she finished her request and her father chuckled at her odd request.

"That's a curious request." He said as he thought over his daughter's request.

Ella chuckled at him, "You'll have to take it on your way and think of me when you look at it." Her father's smile widened as she continued, "And when you bring it back, it means you'll be with it." She finished with a small blush across her cheeks, "And that's what I really want."

Her voice trembled as she spoke the next words, "I want you to come back. No matter what." Her father walked over to hug her and she hurriedly trembled in his arms. Her father hugged her as he held the whole world in his arms. Her caressed her head before speaking, "I will."

He kissed her forehead before letting go of her and he continued, "Ella, I want you to treat your stepmother and stepsisters well." He said in a strict voice. "Even though they may be trying at times."

Ella nodded at him, "I promise."

"Thank you." Her father said as he held her hands in his and looked at her with adoration. "I always leave a part of me behind, Ella. Remember that."

Ella closed her eyes when he spoke the next sentence, "And your Mama's here, too, though you see her not." He glanced around the room as he spoke, "She's the very heart of this place."

Ella's eyes filled with tears as she spoke, "I miss her. Do you?" This caused her father to tremble as he spoke, "Very much." Ella sighed at this and her father kissed their joined hands, as the tears flowed down his cheeks.

This deep but sad moment of the father-daughter duo wasn't as private as they wanted it to be; her stepmother was spying on them through the window. This little bitter sweet moment wasn't something she'd let go off easily.

~~~

The same evening as they waited for the servants to load up her father's luggage in the carriage, her father hugged her for the last time before getting on the carriage. Her stepmother stood on the ends of the staircase alongside her stepsisters. Her father tipped off his hat to her stepmother and smiled at them.

Ella stood next to the carriage, anxiously dreading the moment, but wanting to see him before he left. The carriage started moving and Ella took his hand in hers and squeezed it lightly as a reminder to feel that he was still here for a moment.

As it started moving fast, Ella picked up her pace to follow its rhythm. Her stepsisters and stepmother waved her father goodbye. Her stepsisters called out to remind him of their presents in a loud voice, "Don't forget my lace!" "Also, my parasol."

Ella reached the gates when she heard, "It's for my complexion, which means skin by the way." Ella didn't focus on them as she continued running alongside her father's carriage, wanting to see him just a bit longer. As they rounded the corner along the road, she yelled out, "I love you. Bye, Papa!"

Her father turned around in his seat and waved her goodbye, "I love you, too! Bye!" Just like that her father vanished from her sight.

~~~

Cinderella

Ella looked at the further moving away carriage and her heart ached as she knew she wasn't going to see her father for months to come. She wiped away the tears and sniffed slowly as she tried to calm herself. She looked up to see Lady Tremaine smirk slowly at her and then walk inside. Her stepsisters stood their looking awkward and confused. Ella walked towards them and walked passed through them as they observed carefully.

Lady Tremaine heard her enter and called her out in the living room, "Ella, would you mind coming here for a minute?" Ella was to head to her room to be solicited, she didn't want to interact with anyone but, nonetheless she made her way to the living room. Ella didn't show her over the flow emotions as it was because of Lady Tremaine that her father had to leave so early.

No matter how much Ella tried, she kept weeping as she entered the living room. Lady Tremaine saw her emotional self and called her over, "Come here." She said as she engulfed Ella in her arms and hugged her slowly. She patted her back, "Now, now. We have to be strong." Ella still sobbing nodded at her and wiped her nose with handkerchief. After she cleared her throat, Ella spoke, "Thank you, stepmother."

Lady Tremaine looked at her and said, "You mustn't call me that. Madam will do." She smiled softly at her and Ella was shocked at the confusing behaviour but, she nodded her head. "Okay." Ella replied and looked down.

Ella heard her stepsisters arguing in the hallway and her stepmother placed her hand on hers. She heard Drizella talking loudly, "There's no space for my clothes in the wardrobe." Anastasia smacked her hard on her head, "Yes, that's because your clothes are as big as your head."

Ella's eyes widened as she saw Drizella tugged on her Anastasia's head hard and Anastasia screamed. Lady Tremaine cleared her throat as she spoke, "You see, my daughters they have always shared a room and they can be conflicting sometimes." Ella scrunched her face as she thought of the rooms available in their house. Ella turned to look at her stepmother, "The biggest room in the house other than yours and Papa's is mine. They can share it if" Ella didn't get to complete to sentence as Lady Tremaine clapped her hands together excitedly and spoke, "Wonderful! That's so kind of you to do."

"Meanwhile, I can take the attic-" Ella started off but was cut short by Lady Tremaine, "Yes, the attic! It's perfect for you. It's big and nice." Lady Tremaine stood up, causing Ella to stand up. Lady Tremaine walked over to the table and picked up Ella's sewing materials, Ella followed suit as she didn't want her to damage them. She immediately took it from her hands and looked over to see anything missing.

"Take this with you, too." Lady Tremaine said as she clasped her hands together and smiled at her seemingly. Ella found in odd but, ignored the lingering feeling of hatefulness as she walked out of the living room; her sewing work in hands.

She reached the door leading to the attic and pushed it open with the help of her shoulders. The attic's door opened to reveal an air full of dust and cold. Ella coughed a little as the sudden intake of dust didn't help her breathing. She looked over to see a huge span of dust all over the attic. The spider webs all over the furniture sitting there, "This will take a while." She spoke as she placed the box of sewing materials on the floor and tightened the hair band around her head.

Ella started off first by placing the standing bed neatly on the ground and covered her nose as the dust spread all over the attic due to the placing of the bed. She covered it by using a rug she found in the attic and smiled at her attempt to make attic seemingly better.

She grabbed a broomstick as she swept the dust off the floor and jumped a little as she heard some noises coming over from the table covered in the corner. She walked over slowly, not making any noise as she didn't want to scare them away. She slowly picked up the cloth and almost screamed as she saw Jaq and Gus eating cheese along with other mice on a small pot turned over to serve as a table. Gus looked startled at her sudden appearance and lost his balance as he jumped backwards. But, Ella caught him in time and placed him back on the table, "There, there Gus." She smiled at their small table and patted their heads.

"So, is this where you guys take refugee?" She asked them as she placed her hand on the table and sat down on the floor. The mice nodded their head at her question and continued eating their cheese. She chuckled lightly at their answer, "Well, I guess. It's my refugee too then."

Ella stood up and dusted off her dress and smiled widely, "Let's make it more comfortable, shall we?" Ella danced lightly on her feet as she swept the floor. The mice followed her every movements and tried to help with little things. Ella started singing her favourite song "Sing, sweet nightingale"- the one her mother always sang to her and placed the carpet on the floor.

After she was done tiding the attic, she danced around the attic and said loudly, "How very peaceful."

She looked at the mice and smiled at them as they looked at her with confused expressions. "No cats," She said and the mice jumped excitedly at her. Ella walked over to the door and closed it as she said, "No stepsisters."

~~~

Ella busied herself over the course of days as she waited for father to write her letters on his journey. The letters were a reassurance for her, as her father was still well and doing well. She woke up every day with a bounce in her steps as she knew she was close to seeing her father again.

She helped the maids in cooking and cleaning. She read a new book everyday as she couldn't let her mind just close itself on their small town. She wanted to travel the world with her father, as she believed there were endless possibilities out there in the world and she's like to explore them all. Maybe she'd be able to visit her mother's native country one day, she thought.

Ella used to imagine her mother's country to be full of fairies and beautiful people. She heard the stories about the culture and the golden sand of their deserts. She wanted to see sand with her own eyes and play in it. She felt that she would feel more connected to her mother, as she grew up there. Ella had seen paintings from her mother's room, as to how beautiful their culture was and she wanted to celebrate it. Ella walked towards her Papa's bedroom wanting to take a glance at her mother's painting.

She smiled to herself as she slowly opened the door to her Papa's bedroom. But, her eyes widened as she saw Lady Tremaine taking the hanging painting down from the wall and placing it carelessly on the floor.

"What are you doing?" Ella exclaimed as she rushed into the room and picked it up carefully, trying not to damage it. Ella nearly dropped the painting as she saw a part torn in the corner. The paint coming off the paper and Ella looked at Lady Tremaine's nails and saw the scrappy bits of the paint dangling off them.

Lady Tremaine didn't reply as she just stared at the poor child in annoyance. Ella shook her head as she tried not to cry again in front of her as she only pitied on her, she didn't want to be on the receiving end of this fake pity.

"I...I was just trying to put up my picture instead of this old painting." Lady Tremaine replied as she twirled a wine glass in her hand and looked around. She looked unbothered as she just caressed her own painting, and smiled at it lightly.

Ella was angry as the one thing remaining of her mother was her paintings, and her stepmother tried to throw them away. She was fuming with anger, and tried to control it but, it was too late as the words she sputtered out, "How dare you?"

Lady Tremaine was startled as she hadn't seen Ella raise her voice since she moved here, but she recovered quickly as she turned to look at the fuming Ella, "What?" She scrunched her face as she spoke, "How dare you speak to me like that?"

This shook Ella out of her anger and Ella quickly turned her gaze to the ground. Ells blinked twice to realize where she was standing and looked up to find her stepmother with a smirk on her face, "I..I.. I'm sorry. I didn't mean to shout. It's just that-" But, she didn't get to finish her sentence as Lady Tremaine turned her around with her shoulders and pushed towards the door.

"You should be." Lady Tremaine said as she pushed Ella out of the door and threw the painting next to her on the floor, "Take this piece of garbage with you." She shut the door in her face and left Ella sobbing on the floor with her now more damaged mother's painting.

~~~

A few weeks had passed since her father had left her and Ella was getting more than anxious as he hadn't sent a letter for almost two weeks now. He would send one every week but, she was losing her patience slowly.

After the last week's fiasco, Ella had picked up her mother's painting and collected the remaining ones from her father's office and hung them all in her attic. It was for the better as they wouldn't bother anyone and Ella would feel more close to her mother.

She couldn't stop missing her father as he wished for his health and thought of him in everything she did. Small things reminded her of her father and she smiled fondly at their memories.

Ella scraped her plate as she helped out the maids in the works and swiped the sweat off her forehead. One of the maids, pushed Ella lightly with her hips, "You don't have to work here, Ella. You know that." Ella chuckled at her and said, "Yes, I'm very well aware. But, I love to help." She continued scrapping the dishes as all the maids laughed at her innocence.

After the work, she headed out in the poultry with rice bits in her wooded basket. She opened the door to the poultry and bent down to spread the food around for the chickens to eat. They all gathered around here and she looked fondly at them. She walked over to the nest and picked up two eggs and said, "Thank you, Miss Lily."

As she was about to enter the kitchen again, she heard the bell from the mailman. She placed the basket on the ground and rushed over to the main door, as he would deliver her father's letters.

Excitedly she opened the doors, Lady Tremaine was right behind her, along with her stepsisters. The mailman stood in front of her, with his head bent down and had his hat in his hand. Ella's looked at him in confusion as she didn't expect to see him so gloom.

She searched around him to find any hints as to why he was so gloom but, couldn't. He looked up at her and said, "It's your father, miss." She waited for him to continue and nodded at him, "He took ill on the road, my child." Ella took a sharp intake of breath as she heard the news. She placed a hand on her chest as she tried to calm her beating heart.

"He's passed on, miss." He said in a low voice. Ella took a step back as she heard the news, didn't quite believing him. She shook her head, trying to wake up as she thought it was a nightmare. Just a nightmare.

But, she was brought to reality as the mailman said, "He's gone." He placed a rose in her hand as he looked down, "He asked to give this to you, miss." Ella slowly took the rose in her hand and looked at it with tearful eyes. A tear escaped her eyes and she looked up at the mailman, "He spoke only of you and your mother in his last moments, miss. He loves you dearly." He said as he bowed in front of her.

"Thank you, Mister." Ella said as she tried to smile lightly, "It must have been hard for you. Thank you again." Ella bowed to him and heard him say, "I'm sorry, miss." She closed the door behind her and turned around to find her stepmother screaming, "How will we live now?"

Ella broke down as she cried, mourning her father's death.

~~~

Beast

Lumière laid out the plan on the table in front of them and Mr. Cogsworth looked up at him with confused facial expressions. Lumière looked proud as he was almost sure that his plan would work, even if it didn't at least he would get to see his Master happy and that was enough for him.

Featherduster walked around him as she read the plan and looked in deep thoughts. Mrs. Potts tried to calm Chip's excitement down and smiled lightly at Lumière.

Mr. Cogsworth cleared his throat before speaking, "So, you mean to say Lumière that, we beg Enchantress to turn us into human form for two nights so, we can host a party and Master finds the love of his life?" Mr. Cogsworth looked seconds away from fainting as his head hurt from Lumière's stupid idea.

Lumière nodded at him, placing his hands on his waist, "Yup, that's the plan."

Featherduster sighed at him, "This won't work, my love." This caused Lumière to frown and he turned towards her, "And why do you think so?"

Mrs. Potts sighed loudly, finally loosening Chip from her grip and letting him jump down on the floor, "Because, Lumière even if your plan works. How do we find the Enchantress?"

Lumière looked at Mrs. Potts, "I may have an idea but, I don't know if it will work."

"What is it?" Mrs. Potts asked, suspicious of the plan now, as Lumière tend to go overboard with his plans.

Lumière avoided eye contact with anyone as he paced around the room, and looked down. "I mean...." He started but, didn't complete as he knew no one would agree to it.

"You mean?" Mr. Cogsworth urged him to continue.

Lumière scratched his head, as he turned around abruptly, "ImeanwecanaskMastertotakeustotheEnchantresswiththehelpofthemagicalbook." He shrugged lightly as she finished the sentence in a breath, not daring to look at anyone.

"You what?" Mrs. Potts lashed out as she had heard him correctly and now she was certain that he had lost his mind.

Lumière's expressions crumbled as he looked at them and saw them looking at him, as he had lost his mind, he shrugged at them as he spoke, "We could try."

Featherduster narrowed her eyes at him, "How can you even think of this?" She asked him, "Why would Master agree to this?" As she finished asking her question they heard a new voice speak up, and everyone in the room froze in their spot.

"Why won't Master agree to what?" The Beast asked as he stepped in the room, he had calmed down after yesterday's fiasco and in a good mood seemingly

The servants were scared to death as Master tended to lose his temper at minimal things. The Beast looked around the room but, heard no voice as he waited for a response.

"Mrs. Potts, what is going on?" He asked her, as she was the wisest amongst them. "I..uh..nothing is going on here, darling. You mustn't worry about anything. It's nothing." She nodded at him with certainty even though her heart was beating rapidly.

Mr. Cogsworth's mind had stopped working and he did everything in power to not make eye contact with his Master. Featherduster hid behind Lumière as Master looked around the room for any suspicions. Madame Garderobe was asleep upstairs so, she wasn't aware of this meeting.

"Lumière? Is there something, you wish to tell me?" The Beast asked while looking down at him. Lumière knew there was no other way to let him know about their plans. So, he mustered up all the courage he could and squared his shoulders before looking up at his Master and spoke, "Master, we have a plan for breaking the curse."

The Beast seemed startled as he hadn't thought of this, when he came here due to the commotion. He tried to relax and spoke, "Okay. Go on, what is this plan of yours?" He folded his arms as he stood up straight.

The room was filled with gasps seconds later, as they hadn't expected him to react so calmly. Mrs. Potts stepped forward as she asked him, "Are you sure, Master that you want to hear this?"

The Beast chuckled at her, "What do you think of me, Mrs. Potts? A monster?" He shook his head as he paced the room, with his hands behind his back. "I made the mistake of not listening once and now I'm living its consequences. We don't want to suffer another misery, do we?" He looked at her, smilingly lightly and Mrs. Potts understood his pain.

Mrs. Potts nodded at him knowingly. He turned to Lumière, "So, Lumière elaborate this plan of yours." He walked over and sat at the table and everyone followed suite. Lumière climbed the table and pointed at the plan spread out. The Beast held the paper in his hand, as he looked over the writings and tried to concentrate, but failed miserably as everyone was staring at him with strange eyes and he shivered at their gazes.

"Will everyone just stop staring at me?" He roared out loud and this left the servants shook as they hadn't expected him to burst out.

"Sorry, Master." Mr. Cogsworth spoke softly, and urged him to focus on the plan. The Beast shook his head and continued looking over the pages.

"Elaborate your plan, Lumière." The Beast nodded at him and Lumière bowed down before speaking, "Master, it's quite simple. We travel to meet the Enchantress using the magical book, she gave you." The Beast nodded at him to continue, "Then, we ask her to spare us two nights, just to experience what's it's like being human again, and give us a chance to feel alive again." He shrugged at his Master as he finished.

The Beast looked out the window as he rested his claws against his chin, "Hmm.....alright. Let's see if this works." He said as he got up from his chair and walked towards the door, he stopped as he was about to walk out but, realized that no one was moving.

He turned around to face them, "What's the matter? Don't you want to do this?" He asked them as he looked around the room to find everyone rooted on their spots with their eyes wide open and jaw hanging open.

Lumière seemed to be shaken out of his trauma as he asked the Beast, "You just agreed to do this, just like that?"

The Beast smiled at him with his sharp teeth on display, "Just like that."

~~~

The library was dark with only the candles lit in some places. The servants gathered the Beast as he took the magical book out from the book shelf and placed it on the book stand. The magical book was another gift by the Enchantress to the Beast, the book allowed him to go anywhere in the world his heart desired. But, it was just another curse of the Enchantress, as no one in the world accepted the hideous looking beast and were scared of him.

The Beast looked at Mrs. Potts and smiled before opening the book. He looked at his servants and asked, "Are you ready?" Before placing his palm on the book page. They nodded and placed their palms on the book, along with his and closed their eyes.

For a moment, it seemed as they had entered a black dimension, as there was nothing but, blackness in front of their eyes. The floor beneath them shook lightly and then they opened their eyes.

They were transported to the forest and it was freezing cold, Chip hugged Mrs. Potts tightly as he was afraid. Featherduster squeezed Lumière's hand slightly and he looked at her, nodding that it was okay. Lumière looked up to see his Master trying to find anything unusual in the forest.

The Beast looked down at him and shook his head. Lumière released a breath as he spoke, "Enchantress? Are you there? We have come for a bargain." He finished and shrugged at the Beast when he tapped on his shoulder.

The hustle in the winds increased and the wolves howled loudly around them, the servants were scared and the Beast looked around to find any signs of danger. Suddenly, a light glowed in front of them and the Enchantress arrived. She was just as beautiful as the tragedy night but, the darkness of the night around her made her look hauntingly beautiful.

"Why did you call me here?" The Enchantress asked as she stood in front of them."

"We are here for a bargain." Lumière replied with his shoulders squared, not daring to lose confidence.

"Ohh, silly man. Don't you understand? You can't bargain with me. You are at loss." The Enchantress spoke as she chuckled lightly.

The Beast came forward, "We know, Enchantress. But-" He hesitated for a second.

"But, what? You monster." The Enchantress spat in anger and the heat around her grew. The servants could feel the burns from where they stood.

The Beast hesitated as he knew he was at fault. He was about to answer her question when Mrs, Potts beat him to it, "But, we were humans too. And, we accept that we made a mistake. All we ask for is a chance to be human again." Her answer softened the Enchantress's gaze but, she shook her head as looked at the Beast.

"No!" She declared as she looked at them, "No! You don't deserve kindness."

The Beast stopped Lumière from speaking again as he knew it was pointless to try to convince her and shook his head. They were about to leave when they heard a tiny voice

"Please." Chip said as he walked towards the Enchantress. Mrs. Potts's eyes widened as she realized Chip wasn't with her and shrieked loudly, "No! Chip. Come back, my child."

Chip ignored his mother's calling as he walked towards the Enchantress. The Enchantress was vary of his movements and asked him, "What do you want, child?"

"All I wish it to be able to play with my Mama and Papa as a human for two nights." Chip said as he looked at her with watery eyes.

Everyone gasped as they knew he had crossed a line and were waiting for another curse or a punishment but, were shocked when the Enchantress bent down and caressed him with her hands. She looked at him with adoration and spoke, "Alright."

The Beast's eyes widened as he couldn't fathom the reality, "What?"

"Yes, I will agree to your bargain but, only for two nights. Two nights for you to be human again. After that, you would be in the clutches of the curse again and it will remain the same till the last petal falls." The Enchantress spoke with a strict voice, and everyone nodded at her response.

"Thank you so much!" Lumière said as he jumped in his spot. The Beast smiled at her as he couldn't express his joy through words.

The Enchantress pointed her wand at them and closed her eyes as she cast a spell. The heat around them increased and they closed their eyes, waiting for the transformation. But, they never did transform.

Chip looked at her with confusion, "Why aren't we human?"

"Because, my child the spell will work from the first ray of sunshine." She smiled at him and he smiled back. He ran off towards his mother and jumped up to hug her.

"Oh Chip, you mustn't do that again. Do you understand?" Mrs. Potts said as she hugged him tightly against her chest and showered him with kisses.

Everyone thanked the Enchantress and she smiled at them lightly, everyone except the Beast. They were about to leave when the Enchantress stopped them, "You must remember that if you happen to be alone with someone in the castle for those two nights, the monster's true self will be revealed and the curse can't be broken without true love."

They nodded at her and left the forest, Beast's heart constricted at the thought of being human again and he smiled to himself.

~~~

Cinderella

Ella swiped the sweat from her head with the help of her sleeves as she washed the clothes. Her stepsisters snickered from behind her, as they giggled at her sorry self. Ella paid them no attention as she focused on finishing off this work, so she could take on another.

Her body felt tired as she hadn't been able to sleep well, after hearing her father's demise. The attic was cold too and winter was starting, so it didn't help her cause. Ella finished washing the clothes and threw the dirty water in the drain as she stood up. She put the washed clothes into the drier basket and let the wet one dry in the sun. Her head ached but, she ignored it as she walked outside and started hanging the washed clothes one by one on the rope. She finished hanging them and was about to head to the kitchen when she heard her stepsister Drizella call her name, "Ella! My dear sister."

Ella sighed as she made her way to her sister's room slowly. She couldn't ignore them as her stepmother would be angry with her and she didn't want to upset her anymore as she was still mourning for her father's death.

Ella gasped as she entered her sister's bedroom to find the room messed and covered in clothes with her stepsister Anastasia sitting on the bed, painting her nails and Drizella throwing clothes out of the closet one after the another. Ella looked at Anastasia and asked her, "Why is she throwing all the clothes out?"

Anastasia ignored her question and continued painting her nails. Ella walked inside the room and closer to her sister's closet which once used to be hers. Ella stood next to the pile of clothes and called out her sister, "Drizella, what are you doing?"

She heard a shriek from inside the closet and heard her sister groan as she threw out another corset, "I can't seem to find my blue dress!" Ella blinked twice at her sister's angry voice and tried to calm her nerves. She was startled to say the least.

Ella looked around the heap of clothes to find anything that looked blue. She found one and held it up as she asked, "Is this the one you were looking for?" Drizella stuck out her head from the closet and shook her head, "No! Not this one. I'm looking for the diamond studded one." She backed out the instant she finished speaking but, Ella managed to take a glimpse at the dress she was wearing. Indeed, it was the one she was searching for.

Ella sighed as she knew how naïve Drizella was, but she never spoke it out loud as it would upset her, "Drizella! I found the dress you were looking for." Ella crossed her hands behind her back as she waited for her stepsister to walk out of the closet.

Her sister immediately came out of the closet and looked Ella all over as she tried to find her dress, "Where is it?" She asked, "Why can't I see it? You told me you found it, Ella! Where is it?" She shouted as she was getting impatient.

Ella shuddered at her shouting and tried not to let it show through her expressions, "Ummm... I found it."

Drizella narrowed her eyes at her, "Yes, then when on earth is it?"

"You are wearing it actually." Ella replied with an awkward expression as she didn't want to upset her stepsister.

Anastasia laughed out loud evilly at this and pointed the nail paint brush at her sister, "You dumb idiot." She chucked the pillow next to her at Drizella.

Ella tried to be as silent as she could muster as she didn't wish to be included in their banter. Drizella's face reddened as she looked at Ella and Ella ignored her gaze. Drizella picked up a hairbrush from the dressing table and threw it Anastasia, knocking her nail paint bottle down; causing the nail paint to spill all over her bedsheet.

"Oh no, you didn't." Anastasia said as she jumped over Drizella and they both landed on the pile of clothes. They grabbed each other's hair and started pulling. Ella stood awkwardly in the room as her stepsisters fought over the minimal matter. She sighed as she grabbed the bedsheet and started folding it, for to be washed later.

As she placed it in the basket, her stepmother Lady Tremaine cleared her throat as she entered the room, "Girls!" She exclaimed as she narrowed her eyes at them, "Stop fighting and get ready. We have to go meet the mayor."

The sisters immediately stopped fighting as they heard their mother and stood up. Their stepmother scrunched her face at their dishevelled hair and torn clothes. "Now!" She spoke and they put on whatever clothing they found and straightened their hair.

Once ready, they joined their mother at the door, and Lady Tremaine spoke, "Ella, my dear. Would you clean up the room?" Before Ella could argue anymore she spoke again, "That would be lovely, dear." Thus, making her statement she left with her nose held high in air, full of pride.

Ella sighed as she bent down to pick up the clothes and separated them accordingly. She sat down on the floor as she folded one cloth after the another. Her stepmother had fired every one of their servants as after her father's death, they couldn't afford to pay them. Ella with tearful eyes had bid every single one of them goodbye. When she entered the house again, it felt odd as she was used to the continuous hustle all around the house since she grew up.

So, Ella took it upon herself to maintain the liveliness of the house and started working. She woke up early daily to start off the day by cooking breakfast for everyone, then she washed all the dishes. After cleaning the kitchen, she would head to the living room and tidy up the mess created by her dear stepmother and stepsisters. Her day consisted mostly of cooking food, cleaning the mess and doing things for them. Her sisters couldn't tidy their room on their own as they were never taught to do so. Her stepmother on the other hand, created new tasks for her every day and increased her stress.

Ella didn't mind all the mushing as she was still trying to get over her father's death but, the presence of her stepmother reminded her daily and taunted her. Ella shook her head as she continued folding the clothes and after placing them all in the closet, she returned to her attic.

~~~

Ella jumped at the sound of the door closing loudly, her stepmother and stepsisters were gone for the whole day and she was glad to have the house all to herself. She placed the lid on the soup she had prepared and wiped her hands on the cloth. She was about to plate the dinner for them when she heard Drizella shout, "Dinner, Ella."

Ella quickly plated the dinner and picked up the plates and made her way to the dining room, "Coming." She placed them on the dining table and served water to them. She stood there as they ate and served them more food as they asked her.

After they finished eating, she picked up the plates and walked towards the kitchen. She washed them quickly and let them sit to dry. She grabbed some leftover soup and sat down on the ground near the fireplace to warm up from the cold weather.

Gus and Jaq sat next to her as she just moved her spoon around the soup. They looked at her and pushed her hand slightly to catch their attention. She looked deep in thoughts and smiled lightly at them as she looked at them, "Hey there, Gus and Jaq. Did you guys have dinner yet?" She asked them as she stood up and grabbed some cheese and a bowl. She flipped the bowl and put the cheese she grabbed on it before placing the bowl on the ground.

Gus and Jaq stood up on their feet as they grabbed the cheese and munched on it, looking at Ella. Ella just played with her food, before throwing it in the dustbin. Gus looked at her and she said, "It's okay. I'm not hungry." Gus offered her his cheese and she shook her head, laughing at him, "You eat it. I'm full." She nodded at him and washed her own bowl.

She grabbed the blanket and pillow from the attic and placed it in front of the fireplace. It was too cold for her to sleep in the attic and the fireplace in the kitchen was the warmest place in the house. So, Ella made her bed and slept peacefully as she felt warm, almost as if she was in her happy memory, next to her Mama and Papa.

~~~

Ella was woken up from her sleep by her stepmother's loud shriek, "Ella breakfast!" Ella stood fast even though she felt dizzy from just being woken up. She had slept for almost seven hours, the longest she had in a while. It took her a few moments to process reality and washed her hands to start preparing the breakfast. She threw on her apron and put a kettle on the stove.

She whisked up a batter for the pancakes and made tea on the side. After ten minutes and heavy hustling, she had prepared them breakfast. She set it all on the tray and walked out in the dining room. She placed the tray on the table and stood back as her stepmother walked behind her and sat on the table.

Her stepsisters walked into the room and snickered when they saw her. Her hair was all over the place and the ash from the fireplace was smudged onto her face, the dress was ruined due to the dark colour of the ash. Ella tried to smudge out the stain but, failed to do so. Her stepsisters now sat on the table and she served them dinner, she made one for herself and she placed it on the table.

"Who is this fourth plate for? Are we having any guests over?" Her stepmother asked as she looked around the house to find anyone other than them.

"Umm... It is for me." Ella said as she placed her hand on the back of the chair to pull it out herself to sit. But, her stepmother stopped her as she placed her hand on hers and said, "You?" She said it with such disgust that Ella was confused at her behaviour, "How can you sit with us? You are a servant. Go eat in the attic or the kitchen." She said as she looked away from her as her mere presence disgust her.

Ella felt her heart break as she looked at her stepmother, but she knew she had to be strong to make her mother proud. She picked up her plate, and heard Drizella and Anastasia speak, "Yes, Ella. Go away no one wants to eat with you."

"You are just a brown skinned ugly girl, with black ash all over her face." Ella touched her face and there were the ash remains from the fireplace all over her face.

"Where is it even from?" She heard her stepmother ask, "Did you sleep in the kitchen?" She asked her and Ella managed to nod a little. "Good, because that's what you deserve." Anastasia said as she laughed at Ella and Ella couldn't take it anymore so, she ran from the house, throwing her plate away in anger.

It was getting too much for her to handle and she had no one to console her. She ran over to the stable and got on her horse and rode towards the forest. She slapped the rope fast as she rode deeper into the forest. She rode as fast as she felt like going away from her stepmother and stepsisters. She couldn't stand in the same room as them any longer and thus she wanted her peace.

The woods grew thicker as she ventured deeper into the forest, with tears streaming down her face. The air smacked her face as she rode faster and the leaves around her looked greener than usual.

Suddenly her horse stooped and she held on the ropes as to not fall over and she said, "Steady boy, steady." The horse didn't listen to her as he neighed loudly and jumped again. She tried calming him by caressing him slightly. But, she succeeded only a little, the horse kept on moving around here and there. She looked up to see a stag standing in front of them and knew why the horse was acting weird.

"I got it, honey. It's okay." She said as she caressed him.

She looked at the stag and said, "We mean no harm. I won't hurt you. I promise." The stag just looked at her and the horse kept on moving around. All of a sudden she heard a gunshot and her eyes widened as she looked at the stag, looking frightened. She shook her head at him, "You have to go. They'll kill you." The stag didn't budge and kept on looking at her.

She shooed him as she said, "Run! Run!" the stag finally understood what she was saying as they heard another gunshot and he ran away. Ella let out a breath of relief as the hunters won't hurt the stag.

The horse jumped as he saw the stag run away and started running off. Ella tried to calm him down but, he didn't listen to her as he kept on running. She struggled to keep her balance as she tightened her grip on the ropes. She heard someone shout, "Miss!" from the woods and she looked at her side to find a young man riding a horse of his own. He paced his horse at her speed and grabbed the ropes as she slowly stopped the horse.

"Miss, are you alright?" He asked her as they both stood in the deep woods trying to calm themselves.

Ella spoke fast, "I'm alright. But, you've nearly frightened the life out of him." She said as her horse turned around.

"Who?" The young man asked confused as he looked around.

"The stag." Ella spat out as she was angry with the idea of someone hurting animals.

The young man chuckled at her but, Ella continued, "What's he ever done to you that you should chase him about?"

"I must confess that I have never met him before." The young man said smiling at her. "He is a friend of yours?" He asked her as they both turned around in circles on their respective horses.

She smiled at him as she said, "An acquaintance. We met just now." She said as she nodded at the path.

"I looked into his eyes and he looked into mine, and I just knew he had a great deal left to do in his life. That's all." Ella said as she looked at the young man.

The young man's smile widened as he asked her, "Miss, what do they call you?"

Ella shook her head at him, "Never mind what they call me."

He shook his head at her, "You shouldn't be this deep in the forest alone."

Ella chuckled at him as she spoke, "I'm not alone. I'm with you, Mister.." She looked at him, "What do they call you?"

The young man chuckled at her question and asked, "You don't know who I am?" Ella's face scrunched up in confusion as she looked at him. The young man continued, "They call me Adam. Well, my mother used to call me that when she was around." His face deemed as he spoke the last words.

Ella smiled lightly at him, "I'm sorry, Mister Adam."

"It's alright." He said as he looked away from her.

"And where do you live, Mr. Adam?" Ella asked him as she tried to lighten their mood.

Mister Adam smiled at her, "At the castle. I live in the castle. I'm learning the trade there." He said as he nodded his head.

Ella's eyes widened as she asked him, "You're an apprentice?"

Mister Adam looked confused but replied nonetheless, "Of a sort."

Ella smiled at him, "That's very fine. Do they treat you well?" She asked him.

Mister Adam scoffed at her question as he answered, "Better than I deserve, most likely. And you?"

Ella's smiled fell as she replied, "They treat me as they are able." She shrugged at him.

"I'm sorry." Mister Adam replied as he looked at her.

"It's not your doing." Ella looked at him questionably.

He bent down as he said, "It's not yours either, I'll bet."

Ella smiled at him, "It's not so very bad. Others have it worse, I'm sure." Her answer gained her a smile from him.

"We must simply have courage and be kind, mustn't we?" She asked him with a sad face and he replied, "Yes. You're right. That's exactly how I feel." He chuckled lightly as he looked down.

They both heard the royal horn and Ella's eyes widened as she realised what was going on, "Please don't let them hurt him." She begged him.

Mister Adam gestured around them as he spoke, "But, we are hunting you see. It's what's done."

This angered Ella and spat in anger, "Just because it's done doesn't mean it's what should be done."

Mister Adam seemed surprised at her answer, "Right again."

Ella's face reddened at his direct answer and she asked him, "Then, you'll leave him alone, won't you?"

"I will." Mister Adam replied as he looked at her.

Ella smiled at his answer, "Thank you very much, Mister Adam."

Mister Adam was about to reply when they heard a third voice speak up, "Ah, there you are. Your Highn..." Mister Adam stopped him as he spoke loudly, "It's Adam! Adam!"

"Adam! I'm Adam. I'm on my way." Mister Adam replied loudly as he nodded at them.

Mr. Cogsworth smiled at Mister Adam as he spoke, "Well, we better get a move on then, Mister Adam."

Mister Adam looked back at Ella as he said, "As I said, on my way." He smiled at her as he took in her beauty.

He walked his horse back a little as he said, "I hope to see you again, miss." He smiled widely at her.

"And I, you." Ella nodded at him as she smiled.

Mister Adam turned his horse around and tugged on the ropes to run faster. In a moment, he was gone with the wind and Ella turned her horse around as she smiled to herself and rode her horse back to her house.

~~~

Beast

"Come on, work faster." Lumière shouted as he stood with his arms folded over his chest. He looked mad as he knew it wasn't their fault, as they had just become human and it was hard for the servants to get their body to work faster but, he couldn't help but feel that his idea of the ball was going to work out. The worst part of their deal was that the Enchantress had taken their magic away from them and this didn't help their cause. The only bit of the magic was left with Master and he was missing, that's what Lumière thought as he had searched for him throughout the castle.

Mr. Cogsworth walked into the ballroom with Madame Garderobe following suit. Lumière glanced at them and looked back at the servants. "Where have you been? I'm going crazy with all the work around here and everyone is missing!" He exclaimed as he threw his arms in the air to express his frustration.

"We went searching for Master, Lumière." Mr. Cogsworth sighed as he yawned and looked tired. Madame Garderobe didn't say a word as she fell asleep on the spot and was snoring loudly in the broad daylight, she was getting old.

"Well, did you find him atleast?" Lumière asked and continued watching the servants.

Mr. Cogsworth yawned again as he said in a dull voice, "Yes, we did. He was in the woods. Hunting." Lumière smacked his head as he frowned, "Why was he in the woods?"

Mr. Cogsworth shrugged at him, "Hunting. You know how much he loves hunting." Lumière nodded at him as he thought of how all the times his Master went hunting he would get the head of the animal he had shot down and hung it up in his room. Lumière shook Mr. Cogsworth from his sleep, "Cogsworth observe them." He nodded at the servants, "And don't let them stop even for a minute. We have to tidy this place before tomorrow's ball." Mr. Cogsworth's eyes were half open half closed. "Do you understand what I'm saying?" Lumière asked him and he nodded at him as an answer. "Good. I'll be back in some time." Lumière said as he left the ballroom and started walking towards the east wing of the castle.

He ran as fast as he could and as he reached his Master's room he sighed out a huge breath of relief as he heard his Master in his room. He knocked on the door and got, "Come in." as a response.

"Master!" Lumière exclaimed as he entered the room and bowed to his Highness. Prince Adam nodded at him and asked, "What brings you here, Lumière? And why are you out of breath?" He sat on the chairs and swirled wine glass in his hand.

Lumière smiled at his Master as he spoke, "I rushed over here as soon as I heard that you returned from hunting. So, what is it that you caught this time?" He asked him looking over every wall in the room to find no changes. His face scrunched in confusion as all the heads had been taken down from the walls and now only the paintings were hung up.

"Where did all the heads go, Master?" Lumière asked him with curiosity.

He heard his Master sigh as he shook his head, "I took them all down. It's wrong of me to do the killing." He said as he looked out the window.

Lumière's interest perked up as he never heard his Master never spoke such language, "And why is it wrong, Master?" He tried his luck as he knew his Master was hung up in emotions and would mostly speak his heart.

"Because if it's done doesn't mean it's what should be done." His Master replied as he didn't meet Lumière's gaze and a little blush filled his cheeks.

"Oh, is it Master?" Lumière smirked as he spoke and this broke Master out from his mind and he looked at Lumière smiling slightly.

Lumière folded his arms over his chest as he smirked at his Master, "You seem quite happy today, Master? Is it a certain someone?" He asked and his Master shook his head.

"It's no one just, a country girl I met on my way back to the castle." Master still didn't meet his gaze and looked anywhere but him.

"Is she a beautiful girl who may have somehow won your heart over?" Lumière asked him.

Master nodded at him as a response but, didn't say anything as he stood up and made his way over the windows. He placed his hand on the window sill and looked down at the servants working to tidy the castle up before the ball.

"Maybe you won her heart too?" Lumière tried to get more information about this said meet.

Master shrugged at him as he spoke, "Maybe." His eyes looked sad as she turned to look at Lumière, "But, it's no use. As she would run as fast as she can when she sees me in my true self. This outer appearance is just a façade for two days." He said in a low voice as he walked back to the table and poured another glass of wine.

Lumière's heart broke as he heard his Master's words but, he remembered the words he had heard his Master say just a minute ago, "But, what if she is not like that?"

Master's eyebrow scrunched up as he looked at Lumière and asked, "How do you know that?"

Lumière smiled at him as he spoke, "You just told me that, she wants everyone to be kind and courage, right?" His Master blushed at this and replied while scratching his neck nervously, "I never said that she said that."

Lumière gave him a look and said, "Really?" in all seriousness and his Master shrugged at him blushing, "Okay, she said that. Why does it even matter?"

"Because," Lumière started off as he paced the room, with his hands behind his back, "She seems like someone who would love regardless of how their appearance was and is very kind." Lumière explained this to his Master, who just nodded his head at him and muttered an occasional, "You are right."

"See, that is it. She is the one." Lumière exclaimed as he looked at his Master with grin. His Master was happy but, he still had doubts as he asked, "We are still not one hundred percent sure, Lumière."

Lumière thought over ways to find out but, couldn't find any. But, suddenly his Master exclaimed as he stood up, "I know a way!" Lumière looked confused as he saw his Master make his way inside his room and followed suit.

His master searched for something in the drawer and tossed one after another thing behind him as he looked. Finally, he exclaimed, "Found it!"

He turned around with the magical mirror given to him by the Enchantress and all the clocks ticked perfectly in Lumière's mind.

Prince Adam smiled widely at him as he gripped the mirror in his left hand and looked into it as he spoke, "Show me the girl." The glass in the mirror twisted slightly for a second as it gave them a blurred image and Master's smile was swept off his face as he shook the mirror with his hand. It didn't change a thing and he had almost lost all the hopes when the blurred picture cleared to reveal a beautiful brown skinned brunette caressing a horse in a stable.

Prince Adam smiled at him delightfully as he confirmed that indeed she was the one who he had met in the woods. "She is beautiful." Lumière said as he looked at her through the mirror. His master nodded at him and continued looking at her image till the it disappeared.

"Well, now we know for sure that she is the one." Lumière said as he stood in front of his master and smiled at him.

His master seemed sad as the girl wasn't in front of him, so Lumière started making a plan for him, "What if we invite her to the ball?" Prince Adam's eyes widened as he thought the idea over but, he shook his head a moment later, "How can we find her? I don't even know her name." He shrugged at him.

"Hmm...." Lumière thought and spoke, "What if we invite everyone in the village to the ball? She might come to the ball? What do you say?" Lumière asked him with a knowing smile and his Master smiled right back at him, "I mean, we can try." He chuckled as Lumière smiled at him and fisted his palm excitedly.

"Invitation for all the villagers, it is then!" Lumière exclaimed as he left his Master in his bedroom and heard him chuckle at his retrieving self.

~~~

Lumière walked over to the ballroom where everyone was waiting for him and Madame Garderobe was still asleep as always. Mrs. Potts turned towards him on hearing his footsteps and as she saw his smile she asked him, "What is it, Lumière?"

Lumière shook his head as he walked and stood next to Plumette. He circled his arm over her waist and she squealed when he twirled her around and smiled widely as he kissed her.

"What is it, darling?" Plumette asked him as she laughed at his smile.

"We may be human forever!" Lumière exclaimed as he smiled at everyone. Everyone gasped out loud at this and started cheering but, Mrs. Potts was still sceptical as she asked Lumière, "How can you say that, Lumière?"

"Because Mrs. Potts," Lumière said as he pulled her cheeks and she swept his hands away from her face, "Master may have met the love of his life." Mrs. Potts gasped as she couldn't believe the news and hugged Chips tightly. Chip managed to slip out of her hold.

"Is it true?" Chip asked as he walked over to the door of the ballroom and spoke out loud.

"Who are you talking to, Chip?" Mrs. Potts asked as everyone looked towards the door but, couldn't see anyone from where they were standing.

A moment later Prince Adam walked inside the ballroom and everyone's eyes widened as they feared that their Master may have heard their conversation.

Prince Adam kept a serious face as he picked up Chip in his arms and walked towards the centre of the ballroom. No one uttered a word as their eyes followed Master's every movement. As he stopped below the chandelier, Prince Adam spoke, "Yes, it is true, dear Chip." He smiled at him and Chip hugged him tight.

The room was filled with endless laughter and smiles as Prince Adam threw Chip in the air and caught him and looked around the room. His servants were happy after a long time and even though the castle was alive due to the magic all these years but, it never seemed happy.

He placed Chip back on the ground and looked at the decorations around the ballroom. He smiled contently at how beautiful it looked and he knew how happy the girl he had met would be after she saw this ballroom.

He looked around the room as he exclaimed, "Let's make this ball, one of the greatest to be held in a million years." Everyone erupted in cheers around him and the castle was filled with love and happiness.

~~~

Cinderella - I

Ella smiled as she made her way back to her house. The conversation between her and Mister Adam replayed continuously in her mind. She didn't even realise she had reached her house and sat on the horse in front of house for almost half an hour; until her stepsisters almost pushed her down from the horse but, she managed to get a hold of herself.

Her stepsisters had laughed off loudly at her expense and her stepmother had walked out of the house to learn the cause for the noise which was disturbing her beauty sleep. She had glared at her daughters and scolded Ella for wasting her time, she had said, "You pathetic girl. Stop wasting my time and get some work done around the house. Always being lazy." She had scrunched her face in disgust and asked her daughters to follow her. This had damped Ella's mood a little but then she remembered Mister Adam's words, "I hope to see you again, miss." And that one sentence had spread a huge smile on Ella's beautiful face.

She had taken her horse back to the stable and fed him food and water while caressing his skin and murmuring sweet nothings into his ear to calm him down from the running and gain back his strength. After that, she had bluntly ignored her stepmother's insults and clap backs as she worked around the house. Her stepsisters had asked her to tidy their room once again even though she had just done it yesterday. The moment she entered their room, it seemed like a storm had ruined their room and she had sighed and worked her way around the mess.

The smile never left her face as she cleaned the house, fed the animals and the evils in her house. After cleaning the kitchen, she had realised that they were going to be out of groceries soon, so she had to make a trip to the town soon. So, she made her way over to her stepmother's room, she knocked on the door as she asked, "Shall I come in, madam?"

Lady Tremaine scoffed on the other side of the door as she muttered, "Come in." Ella looked down as she entered the room and waited for her stepmother to give her permission to speak.

"What is it?" Her stepmother asked as she cleaned her nails, sitting on the chair, looking unbothered by her presence.

"I wanted money to-" Ella started but she was cut off by Lady Tremaine as she leaned forward and focused on her when the matter of money was involved.

"Why do you need money? Don't we provide you enough?" Lady Tremaine asked as she glared at her, daring her to speak. Ella wanted to scoff at her last question but, she forgave her since, her day was a lucky one and she didn't want to ruin it, so she ignored the question and focused on the important things.

"I wanted money for buying groceries, we are running out of stock soon. So, I was heading to the town to buy them." Ella uttered fast as she wanted to get out of the suffocating room as soon as possible.

Lady Tremaine nodded at her as she stood up from her chair and walked towards her closet. She picked up some coins and placed it in a bag and threw it Ella as she walked back to her chair, "Buy whatever is needed from this. No more than this amount should be spent." She turned around as she picked up a rotten apple from the table and threw it on Ella.

Ella nearly got hit by the apple but, she barely managed to catch it and nodded as she made her way out of the room. She threw the rotten apple in the dustbin and collected her basket from the kitchen as she walked out of the house. She smiled as she loaded the basket on the cart and asked the farmer to drop her to the town's road. The farmer compiled and smiled at her as he turned the cart on the town's road.

Upon reaching the town, Ella made sure to visit her former maid's house. She smiled as she knocked on her door and waited for her to open the door. A moment later, the door opened and the maid smiled as she took in Ella's presence, "Ella! What a pleasant surprise!" She exclaimed as she threw her arms around Ella's neck and hugged her tight. Ella's face lit up as she hugged her friend tightly.

They giggled after they let each other go and her friend grabbed a basket along with her as they made their way to the market place. Ella laughed as her friend told her about her new workplace and how the old couple she works for are always forgetful and love and adore each other. Suddenly her friend stopped, causing Ella to stop as well, "Are you safe in the house, Ella?" Concern spread all across her face as she touched her arm and looked at Ella.

Ella shrugged as she smiled, "Yes, I guess. I mean, I'm alright." She shook her head as her friend's expression didn't change a bit, "You mustn't worry about me. I can manage on my own."

Her friend smiled lightly as she asked Ella, "Why don't you leave the house, Ella? I mean you don't have any family left there." Ella smiled at this and shook her head, "I can't leave the house. The house was built by my Mama and Papa and they spent all their lives there. I just can't leave it. For me, they are still alive in there and they are the beating hearts of the house. They cherished the house and that they are gone, I'll cherish it for them. It's my home."

Ella looked at her with sad eyes and was on the verge of crying but, the moment was broken by the loud royal siren. They both looked in the direction of the sound and rushed to the market place. They panted as they reached the market place and saw a small crowd around the centre pole.

Ella saw as the royal guards sat on their horses with pride and honour and it reminded her of Adam's royal clothes, she smiled as she thought of him. He was the sweetest person she had met; well other than her Mama and Papa, she thought.

She was broken out of her thoughts by the loud announcement of the royal officer, "Hear ye! Hear ye!" He announced as he gained the attention of the crowd but was stopped but the barking of the dog, so he shouted, "Quiet!" The crowd fell into silence as he spoke, "Know, tomorrow night, there shall be held, at the palace, a Royal Ball."

The crowd erupted into cheers as they hadn't seen a royal ball in a long time. The announcer ignored the cheers as he continued, "At said ball, in accordance with ancient custom, the prince shall choose a partner to dance. Furthermore, at the behest of the prince, it is hereby declared that every maiden in the kingdom, be she noble or commoner," He stopped as he glanced over the crowd before clearing his throat, "is invited to attend." The crowd erupted in laughter and joy as he continued, "Such is the command of our noble prince." The crowd went haywire as it was the first time for the prince to invite everyone to the Royal ball, be it noble or commoner.

Ella smiled to herself as she looked down and thought of meeting Mister Adam again within the span of two days.

She hadn't been this happy since she last saw her father and mother. She quickly purchased all the required groceries along with her friend as they discussed going to the Royal Ball. She bid her goodbye after she was done with her work in the market place and headed back home. As soon as she reached the house, she thanked the farmer for dropping her off and rushed into the house.

She placed all the groceries in the kitchen and ran to the living room where her stepmother and stepsisters sat wasting their time and energy. She smiled excitedly as she told them all about the Royal Ball and their ears perked up as soon as she mentioned the Prince and the Royal family. She clasped her hands excitedly as her stepmother stood up from her place trying to calm her nerves.

The evil trio was focused on meeting the prince as her stepsisters said, "Me as a Princess?" and, "I'll lure him in my love trap." Her sisters danced around the room as they imagined their fate.

Ella on the other hand just wanted to meet Mister Adam, the apprentice. Her mother bent down on her knees as she placed her hands on her daughter's laps and said, "One of you will win the Prince's heart and then we can pay off the debt we had before we moved to this backwater." She nodded at them as she smirked, imagined bathing in a tub full of gold. She stood up and turned around as she asked Ella, "What are you standing here for after delivering the news? Go rush to the seamstress and ask her to sew three ball gowns for us." She finished as she admired herself in the mirror and fixed her hair.

Ella's ears perked up at the mention of three ball gowns and she sputtered, "Three? That's really considerate of you." She thanked her stepmother as she smiled at her.

Her stepmother frowned as she turned around and Her stepsisters laughed at her. Drizella snorted as she spoke, "Mother, she thinks that the third gown for her." Anastasia laughed out loud as she bent down and slapped her knee. Her stepmother stopped admiring herself in the mirror and walked towards her, "Let me make this clear you, pathetic girl." She took one step forward each time she took a pause, "One for Drizella. One for Anastasia. One for me." She now stood in front of Ella and placed her hands on her shoulders and levelled herself so, that she could look Ella directly in her eyes, "Understood?" Ella nodded slowly as she gulped but, didn't let her demeanour frighten and dampen her mood.

Her stepmother turned her around as she pushed Ella towards the main door and shouted, "Come on, now quick. Go and order three ball gowns to be stitched by tomorrow morning before the seamstress is burdened by the villagers. Ella ignored her negativity as she headed to the seamstress and ordered the required gowns for her stepmother and made her way back home.

~~~

As soon as Ella reached her home, she headed straight for her mother's wardrobe, as her stepmother had taken all her pretty dresses away from her and she couldn't wear her everyday clothes to the Royal Ball. So, she searched for her mother's favourite dress as she knew it was perfect for the Royal Ball. She found it hidden below all the other dresses in a box in her mother's wardrobe. She pulled it from the box and dusted it to remove the dust.

She coughed a little as the dust filled the air and made it hard for her to breathe. She detected it from both the sides and it only needed a few stitches before it was good to go. So, she grabbed it and made her way to the attic where her sewing material was. She picked up the thread and needle and started sewing as she sat in the attic. Gus and Jaq sat next to her and observed her every move. After she was done stitching the torn parts, she looked for some decorations to add on to her dress. The mice helped her a lot as they picked up small fake diamonds and strings and handed it to her to add it to her dress.

By midnight, she finished the dress and sighed in delight as she looked at it. Her mother would be so proud of her, she thought. She hung it in the back of her small closet as she didn't want anyone to know that she had a dress too. She slept peacefully that night as she dreamt of meeting Mister Adam, the apprentice in the Royal Ball and dancing with him.

The next morning, she woke up with a smile lit on her face and prepared a hearty breakfast for everyone as was in a happy mood. The house was chaos other than her as her stepsisters and stepmother ran all over the house, attempting to get dressed and get their makeup done properly.

Ella helped her sisters get dressed as she helped them get into their respective corsets and gown. Their makeup was done to suit their dress and hairstyle. Her stepmother wore a dark green and black gown along with a bold red lipstick. Her stepsisters gushed to themselves as they got ready, "I'll dance with the prince and make him fall in love with me." To which the other replied, "Why would he dance with you? I'm the better looking one, and I have grace. You just wait." As she smirked and applied her lipstick.

After her sisters were ready, Ella quickly escaped to the attic and got ready on her own. She wore the dress she sewed the day before and tied her hair in a half up half down up do, and wore her dark blue ballet shoes. She applied a light pink lipstick and highlighted her blush using the same lipstick. She smiled as she looked at her reflection. Gus and Jaq looked at her adoringly.

Her ears perked up at the sound of greetings from the main gate and she knew that the carriage was here to take them to the castle, so she made her way downstairs. As she neared the ending of the stairs, she saw her stepmother and stepsisters at the door, leaving the house so she called them out, "Madam," They turned around at her voice and before they could say anything, Ella spoke, "This didn't cost you a penny, I swear. It's my mother's old dress and I sewed it myself."

Her stepmother smirked as she heard her answer and motioned her to come to her, "Come here, dear." Her stepsisters snickered at her as she walked down the remaining stairs. Her stepsisters placed her hand on her shoulder as caressed her shoulder, "Oh darling, you shouldn't have gone to great lengths to make a dress for yourself." She stopped as she glared at Ella and her sweet expressions changed into that of anger and hate, she grabbed Ella's sleeves and Ella's eyes widened as she realised what her intention was and before she could stop her, her stepmother tore her sleeve with her hand, "When you aren't even going to the Royal Ball."

Her stepmother turned around as she spoke, "No one wants a farmer girl at the Royal Ball, you pathetic girl. You deserve nothing in this world."

Ella's eyes filled with tears as she saw her stepmother leave through the main gate and she collapsed on the ground as she sobbed.

~~~

Cinderella - II

Ella stared at the retrieving carriage and her eyes filled with tears, she looked at the teared sleeve of her mother's dress and sobbed as her stepmother had taken her memory of her mother's from her. She collapsed on the floor as she wept and cried her heart out. A moment passed and she heard a knock on her door, the door was half open and she could see the silhouette of the person standing on the other side of the door through her blurred vision.

She immediately stood up as wiped her tears with the back of her hand and straightened her dress a little bit before she walked towards the door. She tried to calm herself and opened the door fully. On the other side of the door, stood an old lady with an old, torn, rough cape all over herself. Her head was bent down but, Ella could see her grey locks from where she stood. She held a stick to balance herself and she looked fragile.

The old woman looked up to Ella and smiled at her with no teeth, her smile was kind and warm. Ella smiled back with tearful eyes and asked her, "How can I help you?" The old woman nodded at her as she took a step forward and almost collapsed but, Ella took a hold of her arm and walked her slowly inside the house. She made her sit in the living room carefully and sat beside her, "Would you like me to do something for you?"

The old woman looked at her and said, "I'd like something to eat. Can you give me something to eat?" Ella's eyes widened as she realised that the old woman had been starving and no one had helped her. She quickly stood up from the sofa and nodded at her, "Yes, of course. I'll find something for you to eat."

Ella rushed to the kitchen and fetched some bread and fruits on a plate and walked back to the living room. She handed the old woman the plate and sat beside her as she ate the bread and the fruits as she hadn't had any food in days. She took a huge bite of the apple and turned to Ella, "Do you have any milk?" Ella nodded at her quickly and rushed to the kitchen to bring a glass of milk. She filled a big glass of milk and gave it to the old woman when she reached the living room. Ella stared at her with widened eyes as she saw the old woman gulp the glass of milk in one go and Ella asked her, "Do you want anything else?"

The old woman shook her head at Ella's question and placing the plate on the sofa, she stood up, causing Ella to stand beside her and help her if she lost her balance again. But, this time, the old woman refused Ella's help as she stood up straight on her own and Ella's face scrunched in confusion as she stared at the old woman. The old woman's demeanour was of a young girl and not some old woman. She turned to face Ella and spoke, "I'm your fairy godmother."

Ella looked at her as she had seen ghost and said, "They don't exist in real life. That stuff is only for children and fairy tales." Ella shook her head at her and took a step back. The old woman chuckled at her and took a step forward, "No, dear. We do exist. We are real." She smacked her head as she realised something and said, "Of course, it's this hideous costume. This is why you don't believe me." She turned sideways and closed her eyes as Ella stared at her as she was speaking rubbish, she opened her left eye and said, "Just give me a second, darling. Let me slip into something comfortable."

The old woman threw her stick in the air and the stick twirled in circles as it went up in the air. As the stick fell back, it created a blue hue of stars and fog and engulfed the old woman. Ella's eyes widened as she stared at the weird happenings in her house and she pinched herself to confirm that she wasn't dreaming. The fog disappeared in an instance and the old woman caught the stick in her hand. As she turned around, Ella couldn't believe her eyes as she stared at a young beautiful woman and not an old woman. She had a gorgeous silver ball gown on with studded diamonds and silver jewellery. The stick had turned into a wand of glass and it sparkled as the fairy godmother waved it around.

Ella's gaze was broken by the fairy godmother as she spoke, "So, do you believe me now?" Ella was dumb folded as she could do nothing but nod at her. The fairy godmother nodded at her as she held the magical wand in her hands, "Good, now we have to hurry. We don't have enough time."

Ella stared at her with wide eyes as she asked, "We don't have time for what?" The fairy godmother shook her head as she walked outside in the garden and searched everywhere, "For the Royal Ball, dear. You wish to go, right?" She asked her as she almost ran around the garden. Ella quickly nodded her head, "Yes, yes! I do!"

The fairy godmother smiled at her enthusiasm, and looked at her as she spoke, "Now, we are looking for something that says 'coach'." Ella looked around the garden and her gaze fell on a trough and she pointed at it, "Oh, that trough?" Her fairy godmother's face scrunched up as she said, "Doesn't really say 'coach'." She looked at the vegetables growing in her garden and said, "No, no. I'm liking fruit and veg." She stepped forward and turned around as she asked, "Do you grow watermelon?"

Ella shook her head as she answered, "No."

"Cantaloupe?" The fairy godmother asked.

"I don't even know what that is." Ella shrugged at her.

"Artichoke?" Ella shook her head no again.

"Kumquat?" Ella had no answer to her questions as she didn't knew about the fruits and veg her fairy godmother was asking about.

"Beef tomato?"

Ella shook her head as she looked around feeling awkward, but then she remembered, "We do have pumpkins."

They made their way towards the pumpkins as her fairy godmother spoke, "Pumpkins? This will be a first for me." She shrugged as she said, "Always interesting."

The mice followed them around as they reached the pumpkin field. Her fairy godmother began, "I don't usually work with squashes." She scrunched her face in disgust, "Too mushy."

The fairy godmother looked around the field as she searched for the perfect pumpkin and her gaze fell upon a big pumpkin, "Let me see. That'll do. Yes. Perfect." She walked towards it as she asked Ella, "Knife?"

Ella quickly picked up the knife from the equipment kept along the side-lines and handed her the knife, "There you are." Fairy godmother took the knife from Ella, "Thank you, darling." She handed Ella her magical wand and bent down to cut the pumpkin from its veins. Ella seemed astounded as she stared at the magical wand in her hand and heard her fairy godmother say, "Hello, my strangely orange vegetable friend." The magical wand in Ella's hand sparkled and Ella took a step back. The fairy godmother spoke, "Just a little snip." As she cut off the veins and exclaimed, "Lovely."

Fairy godmother bent down to pick up the pumpkin and as she picked it up, she gasped out loud, "Heavy pumpkin." She nearly lost her balance but, managed to turn sideways as she tried to place the pumpkin down on the ground. The mice were standing there and would have been smashed if Ella hadn't warned them, "Look out, mice!" The fairy godmother almost threw the pumpkin on the ground but, placed it roughly on the ground. She straightened up as she blew a breath, "Well. Never mind." She smiled as she looked around and nodded her head, "Let's do it here." She walked towards Ella and took the magical wand out of her hands. Ella was still confused as to what was going on, "Do what here?"

The fairy godmother replied nonchalantly, "Turn the pumpkin into a carriage." Ella stared at her as she had lost her mind. The fairy godmother avoided her gaze as she pointed her magical wand at the pumpkin, "You're making me nervous, actually."

Ella asked her, "Shall I shut my eyes?"

The fairy godmother replied, "It might be better." Ella covered her eyes with her hands and fairy godmother grumbled, "For heaven's sake. Let's just go for it." She swished her magical wand in front of the pumpkin and cast a spell. The magic spiked a gold hue on the pumpkin and then it disappeared. The fairy godmother frowned at it but, then suddenly the gold hues returned and the pumpkin started glowing as it grew bigger in size.

"Well, something's definitely happening." She said as she circled the pumpkin. Ella sat at the bench near the field and her fairy godmother sat next to her as she spoke, "You see what the trick is..." Ella looked at her as she stressed her mind to remember, "Actually, I've forgotten what the trick is." Ella chuckled at her as they both looked at the enlarging pumpkin.

Ella's eyes widened as she asked, "I just thought, that if it gets much bigger. ." But, she didn't get to finish the sentence as the pumpkin almost engulfed the bench where they sat and they were crushed between the bench and the pumpkin. They moved around as they ran from the bench, Ella asked, "Is this what you meant to do?"

Fairy godmother scowled as she said, "Do you think that's what I meant to do?" They ran towards the heaps of wheat bundles and fairy godmother shouted, "Takd cover, darling." They both hid behind the heaps as they saw the pumpkin enlarge and burst open in the air. The little pieces of the pumpkin came together as the gold hue engulfed the air and magic sparkled across the pumpkin as it slowly turned into a carriage.

Ella stood up as she saw the golden hue settle on the top of the carriage in the form of design and the carriage was golden and shined like a diamond. The wheels were just as gorgeous as the carvings on them were intricate and beautiful. "There. One Carriage." Fairy godmother said. Ella was stunned as she stared at the beautiful big carriage and said as she smiled widely, "You really are my fairy godmother."

Fairy godmother chuckled at her as she spoke, "Yes, of course, darling. I don't go transforming pumpkins into carriages for anybody." She walked out from behind the wheat bundles and said, "Now. Where are those mice?" Ella quickly followed her footsteps as she said, "Mice?"

"Yes, mice." The mice were standing at the end of the field and ran off as they saw fairy godmother approaching them. "Mice, mice, mice." But, before they could escape, fairy godmother swirled her wand and cast a spell, "Bibbidi-bobbidi-boo!" The spell hit the mice as they jumped around trying to run away. Ella gasped as she saw their ears grew bigger and so did their body transform into horses. Four of them neighed as they adjusted to their new form and Ella rushed to caress them, "Gus, Jaq, oh how fine you look!"

The fairy godmother smiled at her as she said, "Four white chargers." Ella turned to look at her as she asked, "But, how did you..." Fairy godmother looked around as she mumbled, "Now, where are we?" She looked around the garden as she counted, "Carriage, horses...Footmen!" She exclaimed.

"Footmen?" Ella asked still feeling as though she was in a dream.

Fairy godmother's eyes fell upon the two lizards crawling near the well and she greeted them, "Hello, lovely Mr. Lizard." She cast another spell as she pointed the wand at them and spoke, "Bibbidi-bobbidi-boo!" She smiled nervously as she stared at the transforming lizards. The lizard's legs grew larger and their head's changed into similar to human head. The lizards enlarged to human size and they wore the uniform of the Footmen. They crawled as they adjusted and their tails grew smaller as they muttered a simple, "Hello!"

As they finally transformed, the tails disappeared and they bowed in front of them, "You called?" Ella smiled at him as a greeting and heard the fairy godmother mutter, "Now, I need that coachman." Ella looked around as she asked, "Coachman?"

Fairy godmother's eyes widened at her question and replied quickly, "Did I say 'coachman'? I mean 'goose'." She uttered as she swirled her wand at the walking goose and the goose sprung into the air and turned into a coachman. The coachman's nose was still similar to the goose's beak and the coachman landed on the wheat bundle.

He held up his hands in the air as he said, "I can't drive. I'm a goose." Ella laughed as she tried containing her happiness. Fairy godmother called everyone towards the carriage as she shouted, "Now, shoo!"

"Everyone into place, no time to be lost!"

She rushed everyone to the carriage as she uttered, "Come on." They ran towards the carriage as quickly as possible but, Ella halted in the middle as she gasped, "Fairy Godmother!" She bent down as she drew in breaths and looked upto see her fairy godmother turn around, "Yes, what?"

Fairy godmother walked back to Ella and Ella gestured at her dress, "My dress. I can't go in this dress." She looked at her fairy godmother as she asked, "Can you mend it?"

Her fairy godmother sputtered in disbelief, "Mend it?" She gestured with her hands as she looked at her dress, "No, no. I'll turn it into something new."

Ella shook her head as she spoke, "Oh, no. Please, don't." She held her dress in her hands, "This was my mother's." She smiled as she looked down and admired the dress, "And, I'd like to wear it when I go to the palace." Fairy godmother looked at her with no expression." It's almost like taking her with me."

The fairy godmother nodded her head at Ella, "I understand. Do you mind if I gee it up a bit?" She gestured nervously as she didn't want to offend Ella. "Wouldn't mind a nice blue?"

Ella shook her head no as she smiled. Fairy godmother swirled her wand slowly and a string of magic shot Ella's dress and a royal blue hue circled her as the dress fluffed up. Ella twirled around as the dress turned blue and butterflies flew around her, settling around her neckline. Her torn sleeve was fixed and her hair was made in a half up half down style. The gown was the most beautiful dress Ella had ever worn and she felt like a princess. "It's beautiful." Ella gasped as she looked at her dress and smiled at fairy godmother.

"There." Her fairy godmother smiled at her feeling proud. Ella's face was lit with a huge smile, "Thank you for this and everything." Fairy godmother shook her head as she rushed Ella to the carriage. Everybody was already waiting in their respective positions. All, Ella had to do was get in the carriage.

As Ella placed her foot forward to get in, fairy godmother stopped her as she gasped, "Just a moment. Are these the best you have?" She asked as she motioned at Ella's torn shoes. Ella nodded her head as she spoke, "It's alright. No one will notice them anyway. I can manage to hide them with the dress." Ella moved forward to get it but, fairy godmother interrupted her, "We can't let you off like this. I'm rather good at shoes." She said proudly as she twirled her wand and said, "Special shoes for a special princess."

Ella glanced down as she saw the magic create shoes for her. The heeled shoes were made of glass and sparkled like magic and diamonds. Ella shook her head, "I'm no princess." Fairy godmother disagreed as she shut Ella's mouth with her hand, "You are for tonight. Off you go, now."

Ella lifted her legs to look at her new shoes and gasped at the sight of them, "They are made of glass?" Fairy godmother smiled at her cheekily and helped her get in the carriage as Ella was left wondering about the events of the evening. "You'll find them really comfortable."

"Fairy Godmother?" Ella asked nervously, "My stepmother and the girls?" Fairy godmother chuckled lightly, "Don't worry. I'll make sure they don't recognize you." She cast a spell on Ella. Fairy godmother closed the door to the carriage and motioned Mr. Goose to start their journey. Ella stuck her head out from the small window and smiled at her, "Thank you for everything, Fairy godmother. I'll forever be grateful."

Fairy godmother smiled at her adoringly but, then her smile changed into a frown as she realised something and she stopped the moving carriage, "Wait. I almost forgot." She said as she nervously gulped, "Remember, the magic will only last so long. With the last echo of the last bell, at the last stroke of midnight, the spell will be broken and all will return to what it was before."

Ella asked as she smiled, "Midnight?"

"Midnight." Fairy godmother nodded quickly.

"That's more than enough time." Ella said with a heart-warming smile.

"Off you go, then." Fairy godmother replied as she took a step back from the carriage and yelled, "Goosey, go!" It was the first and the last time, Ella saw her Fairy godmother and she felt lucky to be able to meet her.

Thus, Cinderella finally made her way to the castle.

~~~

Beast / Cinderella

Beast's POV

Prince Adam stood in the balcony as he saw the servants working to add the finishing touches to the ballroom. The candles on the chandelier were being put up and curtains were opened as they flared out the designs on them. The ballroom was decorated to its extent as the lamps were lit all around the ballroom. The castle was decorated with lights and beautiful pieces of sculpture, as fireworks were fired to greet the oncoming guests.

Mrs. Potts sat beside Prince Adam as they greeted the incoming guests from the balcony. Mrs. Potts smiled as she nodded and welcomed the guests, but Adam seemed nervous as he looked at the entrance. The guests were lined up behind one another as the Royal announcer announced everyone's arrival and let them in the ballroom. Mrs. Potts turned to Adam, "What is it, darling? You seem to be somewhere else?" She nodded at him to answer but, he shook his head as he spoke, "It's nothing. I'm not nervous." He turned towards the entrance and heard the announcer announce, "Welcome, Lady Tremaine and her daughters, Drizella and Anastasia."

Adam saw as a middle aged woman in a black and green gown, bowed to him and her two daughters followed suit. The announcer spoke, "Drizella, the clever one and Anastasia, the beautiful one." Adam smiled lightly at them as he turned to Mrs. Potts who stared at him, "What?" He asked her, as fear crept inside him.

Mrs. Potts shook her head as she smiled at him, "It's that girl from the forest, isn't it?" Adam choked as his widened, "No, no." Mrs. Potts narrowed her eyes at him and he compiled, "Alright, fine. She's the one I'm looking for." Mrs. Potts's expressions turned serious as she asked him, "What is so special about her anyway? She's just a mere country girl, not a princess."

Adam turned to her as he defended, "She's not just a girl, Mrs. Potts. She's special. There's something about her and she's better than any princess I have ever met." He smiled as he thought of her and blush filled his cheeks. He looked down as he avoided Mrs. Potts's gaze. Mrs. Potts chuckled at his shyness and said, "I get it now, darling. She's a special girl." She nodded at him as he looked up and gave him her approval.

Lumière rushed around the ballroom as he ordered the servants to recheck the guest lists and invitations as he wanted the night to be perfect for his Master. He walked towards the hallway as he searched for Cogsworth, only to find him sleeping on a chair at the end of hallway. He huffed out in anger as he shrieked, "Cogsworth, tonight is such an important night for us and you are sleeping here! Get up, fast." He hit the chair with his legs and Mr. Cogsworth woke up startled. He looked around as he tried to make sense of his surroundings and frowned when he looked at Lumière, "Lumière? You are a human again? How is this possible?" Lumière smacked his head in frustration as he shook Mr. Cogsworth by his shoulders, "Wake up, Cogsworth. We have a lot to do tonight." Mr. Cogsworth frowned but, nonetheless stood up from the chair, and walked alongside Lumière towards the ballroom.

They reached the ballroom and Lumière stopped in his tracks as he looked at Plumette. She looked gorgeous in a white ball gown with her hair tied up in a bun. She stood in front of Lumière with a smile lit on her face and she giggled a little as Lumière rushed to her and swept her off the floor and twirled her around in the hair. He placed her back on the ground and kissed her passionately. They adored each other as they pecked each other lightly.

Someone cleared their throat from behind them and Lumière's eyes widened as he realised his Master was standing behind and they both quickly bowed as Lumière apologized, "My apologies, Master." Prince Adam shook his head at him and said, "It's alright, Lumière. Now, let's get this ball started, shall we?" Lumière grinned at his Master's enthusiasm and nodded at him, "Yes, of course."

Lumière walked towards the centre and clapped his hands in the air, signalling the announcer to commence the Royal Ball.

~~~

Ella's POV

Ella looked out through the windows of her carriage as she left her house. She saw the road ahead of her and smiled as she realised, she was one step closer to meeting Mister Adam, all thanks to her fairy godmother. She was still bewildered at the fact, that she a mere country girl had a fairy godmother. She smiled at Mr. Goose as he asked, "Are you alright back there, Miss Ella?" She uttered slowly, "Yes, Mr. Goose." He nodded at her as he paced the carriage and fastened their speed.

Ella sat nervously in the carriage as they made their way to the castle. In a moment, they reached the gates of the castle and Mr. Goose stopped the carriage. Ella turned towards the door and Mr. Lizard opened the doors as he placed his hand forward to assist her. She smiled at him as she gently placed her hand in his and took a step down from the carriage. As she placed her feet on the ground, Mr. Lizard let go of her hand and closed the doors of the carriage.

Ella stepped forward as she saw the glowing castle and the fireworks. Her gaze followed the beauty of the castle and the place and dread filled her chest. She nervously spoke, "I'm scared, Mr. Lizard."

Mr. Lizard was startled by her sentence and walked next to her more nervous than her as he asked, "Why?"

Ella smiled nervously at him, "I'm just a girl, not a princess."

"And I'm just a lizard, not a footman." Mr. Lizard replied as he shrugged at her and smiled a little to lessen the tension, "Enjoy while it lasts."

Ella nodded at him as she walked towards the staircase and put her step forward, her mother's words ringed in her head as she climbed the stairs hurriedly, "Have courage and be kind."

She reached the castle and rushed towards the ballroom as she heard the announcer, "Your Majesty, Your Royal Highness, my lords, ladies and gentlemen, distinguished visitors and people of our land, the prince shall now choose his partner for the first dance. Let our ball commence!"

She reached the ballroom and knocked on the door, waiting to open, as she entered the ballroom, she heard voices but, as she neared the balcony, the crowd fell into a silence as every eye in the rom turned towards her and she nervously gulped as she made her way down through the stairs.

She bowed in front of them as she reached the end of the staircase and smiled graciously. She saw someone walk in front of her in her peripheral vision and her smile widened as she saw Mister Adam, standing across her with a smile lit on his face.

~~~

"The Magical Night"

Third Person POV

Ella smiled as she looked at Mister Adam and he grinned back at her. She forgot that she had a crowd surrounding her and descended the stairs as she walked towards him.

The crowd parted the way as their Prince walked towards the centre of the ballroom and stared as they both walked towards each other. Ella graciously walked and sighed a breath of relief as she met Mister Adam at the center of the ballroom, under the beautiful chandelier.

They smiled nervously at each other as they stood in front of each other, both in awe of each other. Ella gulped as she started, "Mister Adam." He grinned at her as he looked into her eyes and said, "It's you, isn't it?"

She nodded at him as she looked around the ballroom, only to find every pair of eyes on them. She nervously turned to him as she spoke, "They are all looking at you."

Prince Adam shook his head as he chuckled lightly, "Believe me. They are all looking at you." He cleared his throat before speaking, "Your Highness, if I may, that is," He gulped as he gathered his will to ask her, "It would give me the greatest pleasure, if you would do me the honor of letting me lead you through this...the first...." He stopped abruptly as he feared the idea of rejection but, Ella smiled at him, as she asked, "Dance?"

Realization dawned on him as he vigorously nodded his head, "Yes, dance." He chuckled lightly, nervousness adamant in his mind, "That's it." She answered his question by nodding and that was all it took for Prince Adam to gain his confidence back.

He looked at her with adoration as he circled his right arm along her waist and pulled her closer to him. Ella gasped as she didn't expect him to be so straightforward. She steadied herself as she waited for the music to begun. Prince Adam held his left arm behind his back as they both started moving lightly to the rhythm of the music. He moved her to his left as she twirled and drew her closer again as he placed his left wrist under her right wrist and moved it slowly to the music. They moved to the right as they danced and Prince Adam twirled Ella around.

She smiled at him delightfully and they both forgot about the crowd surrounding them and got lost in their own world, where only they both existed. He moved back as he held her right hand and they danced around the ballroom. Ella's footsteps followed his and it felt like they had been dancing like this forever. He let go of her hand and she circled around herself and held it quickly as she straightened. He drew her closer and she didn't expect to be so close to him tonight and gasped at his moves. He grinned at her lightly and she smiled back. He held her close as they danced.

Ella's gown flowed around her like a shadow as it mimicked her every step and made her look beautiful even more. The crowd gasped as they danced flawlessly and awed in wonder at the pair. They twirled around the ballroom graciously, holding each other's hands and not letting go.

Mrs. Potts and Lumière smiled at each other as they awed at their Master. Their Master seemed happy than ever and they wanted nothing more in this world than seeing him happy. Lady Tremaine tried to look as happy as she could but, she was glooming with anger on the inside as she didn't know who the mysterious girl was.

Prince Adam smiled at Ella as he twirled her, letting her go and circled her. He drew her closer again and moved along the music. Ella gasped as he held her by her waist and picked her up graciously and sat her back on the ground. The crowd awed at their synchronised moves and they clapped as he dipped Ella down, announcing the end of the first dance. They let each other go as they stood apart and bowed down to pay each other respects.

Anastasia looked at Ella with jealousy as she asked Lady Tremaine, "Who is that, Mama?" Lady Tremaine hissed as she replied, "I'm not exactly sure, but this does not bode well." Anastasia scrunched her face as she said, "That's a lovely dress she's got on." Drizella finished her sentence, "And how pretty she is." Lady Tremaine smacked their head with her hands as she nearly shrieked, "Concentrate!" The daughters turned around to face their mother and their mother furiously looked at them, "You must turn the prince's head, you fools! Now, get out there!" She said as she pushed them onto the dance floor. They frowned as they said, "But, no one's asked us to dance yet."

Lady Tremaine announced, "Gentlemen." As she looked at the men surrounding them and captured their attention, "May I present my daughter, Anastasia, Drizella." She pushed her daughters towards the men and the men compiled as they greeted them with, "Mademoiselle." They kissed their hands as Lady Tremaine pushed them, "Off you go!"

The music changed from a slow rhythm to a fast one and the crowd made their way to the dance floor in pairs. Every person stood in front of their partner and bowed before they started dancing to the music.

Ella and Prince Adam smiled at each other as they danced to the rhythm of the music in the centre of the dance floor. The crowd cheered as they music changed and awed at the moves of the people. Lady Tremaine's voice could be heard from the crowd as she cheered, "Smile!"

Prince Adam said to Ella as he twirled her around, "Come with me." Ella happily complied as they both made their way to the door adjoining the ballroom as the crowd parted way for them. They ran as they entered the room and Ella laughed out loudly as she said, "So, you're the prince!"

Prince Adam scratched his neck nervously as he said, "Well, I'm not "the" prince. There are plenty of princes in the world." He said nervously as he stared at Ella's back who admired the paintings on the wall, "But, you can say, there's one thing that makes me special." He scrunched his face as he looked at his hands and saw fur growing slowly and his hands turned into claws. His body grew larger in size as his body weight grew and the fur engulfed his whole body. His legs changed and so did his head, he realised as he caught his reflection in the mirror. He growled at the curse and waited for Ella to turn around.

She smiled as she turned around but, her smile quickly faded as she took in the living monster in front of her. Her eyes widened as she gasped at his figure. She took a step back as she feared for her and looked everywhere to find Mister Adam. But, she didn't see him anywhere.

Adam took a step forward as he reached out for her hand but, she took two steps back away from him. He saw fear and dread in her eyes as she stared at the monster in front of him and he retrieved from her. Ella blinked her eyes as she wasn't sure what she was seeing as the day wasn't weird enough, first the fairy godmother and now this monster.

Ella tried to look for a door to escape but, the one she saw was exactly behind the monster and she knew she couldn't outrun him, so she ran in the opposite direction. She saw a door in her peripheral as she ran absent-mindedly. She heard the monster run after her and she quickened her pace. She held the ends of her gown in her hands and made a move for the door.

Adam frowned as he realised that she was scared but, the monstrous nature overgrew his calm mind and growled loudly as he followed Ella out of the room.

Ella managed to get out of the room but, she ended up in another one and tears formed in her eyes as she realised she had no way out. She turned around slowly as she heard the monster stop and she made sure to not look him in the eyes. She took a step back as the monster walked closer to her and she gasped as her back collided with the wall. The monster trapped her in between his body and the wall. Ella looked down as she closed her eyes and waited for death to come to her. A moment passed and Adam groaned lightly as he looked at her fearful expression and his anger grew.

He banged his claw next to her head and she startled at his action. She opened her eyes and looked at him with fearful eyes. Her eyes widened as she looked at the hole in the wall where he banged his claw. Tear started flowing through her eyes as she looked at him and he took a step back as he heard her mumble, "Mister Adam, where are you?"

Ella placed her palm on the wall and she accidently opened a latch as she fell back, the wall sliding behind her. She shrieked loudly as she tried to hold on to something, and someone caught her. She expected to find Mister Adam when she looked up but, was startled when she saw the claw holding onto her. She let go of the hand as she fell on the ground. She crawled back as she realised she accidently opened a secret room. She quickly scrambled to her feet as she saw the monster enter the secret room, the light from the outside room creating a more frightening shadow.

She looked around her and found a vase lying on a table, she picked it quickly and as she saw the monster approach her, she swung the vase at him, hitting him in the shoulders, the vase broke into tiny pieces and the monster growled at the pain. He stepped back as he held onto his injury and when he looked up, Ella's stopped breathing as she saw the rage in his eyes. He ran towards her with his claw in the air and as he neared her, Ella fell down and she heard him stop. Ella's head pounded as she looked up at him. She blacked out after she heard Mister Adam speak, "Are you alright?"

~~~

Cinderella

Ella gasped out loud as she woke up and smiled in relief as she stared at the ceiling, I'm still at home, thank heavens it was just a dream, she thought. She blinked and stared at the ceiling and thought of her weird dream. She chuckled lightly at the hallucinations she was having, since the ceiling didn't look like the one in her attic. A second later, she frowned as she sat up and looked around the room, this is definitely not my attic, she thought. She looked down expecting to find her daily clothes but, instead she saw her mother's dress whose sleeve had been torn by her evil stepmother. She pinched herself to make sure she wasn't dreaming and reality dawned on her when the pinch stung her arm.

She quickly gathered herself as she got down from the bed and looked around the room, it was a large bedroom with a queen size bed and the decorations looked expensive and classic. She walked towards the window and her eyes widened as she stared at the distance between her room and the ground. She stumbled back and fell on the floor as she tried making sense of things.

She had seen a monster and her fairy godmother last night and as fairy godmother said, the magic would only last so long and everything will be back to its original by midnight, that explained her clothing. But, she still wasn't sure of the monster she had seen. The monster she had seen was just an imagination, right? She thought to herself as she glanced around the room and realised she was still in the castle.

Ella frowned as she heard some snoring and her eyes widened as she heard another person in the room, she gulped slowly as she was scared to look at the other person in the room. She closed her eyes as she turned her head and she peeked through her left eye, anticipating for the monster to jump on her out of nowhere but, she scowled as she saw no one. She stood up and dusted her dress and walked towards the source of snoring. She reached the wardrobe and heard no movement. She placed her hand on the drawer knob and opened it roughly only, to find pieces of clothing folded inside neatly.

She blinked as she retreated back but, stopped in her tracks as she heard a soft cough, coming from behind the dressing table. She grabbed a heavy metal decorative piece kept on the table and walked towards the dressing table slowly, not daring to make any noise. She held the piece in her hand in an attacking position and as she neared the dressing table she saw some movement and immediately hit it hard and let the piece fall down. She heard crying of pain as she searched to find a person but, instead she found a candle stand lying on the ground. Her eyes widened as she saw the candle stand get up and stand in front of her. She grabbed the decorative piece lying on the floor and hit the candle stand again with it. She frowned as she heard, "Oh, you're quite strong. This is a great quality." She stumbled back in horror as she saw the candle-stand stand up and it had facial features like a man and the body too. He lit the candle on his head as he looked up and used the it to light the candles on his hands.

Ella gasped as she asked, "What are you?"

The candle-stand man smiled up at her as he spoke, "I'm Lumière!" He replied enthusiastically bowing in front of her.

"And you can talk?" Ella exclaimed as she looked at him.

"Well of course, he can talk. It's all he ever does." Ella heard a new voice and she turned towards the said voice and saw a clock walking towards her, huffing lightly as it talked slowly.

"Lumière, as the head of the castle, I request you to help her." The clock said as he approached Lumière and stood beside him. Ella turned to look for another weapon but, she found only one small plate nonetheless she picked it up, ready to fight.

She heard Lumière whisper to the clock, "What do you want to be for the rest of your life, Cogsworth? Trust me on this." He turned to Ella as he said, "Come on, miss." Ella struggled to make a decision as she wanted to run away as far as possible but, also follow them out. She decided on the later as she was unaware of the ways to get out of this castle and it would be helpful for her to look around. She threw the plate on the bed as she followed them out, wiping the sweat of her palm on her dress.

The trio made their way out of the room and walked along the corridor, Lumière- the candle stand man turned towards her and she picked him up in her hands, she looked at him as he spoke, "You must forgive first impressions. I hope you are not too startled."

Ella scoffed as she replied, "Why would I be startled? I'm talking to a candle."

Lumière turned his head as he corrected her, "Candelabro, please. You know there's a difference. But, consider me at your service. The castle is your own now, so feel free to go anywhere you like." He concluded as he nodded his head a little.

The clock walking in front of them stopped and turned around as he held his clock hands in the air and said, "Except the west wing."

Lumière moved his hands to indicate a no and shook his head as he tried to look calm. The clock continued further on, "Uh, which we do not have."

"Why?" Ella asked as she looked in between the two of them. "What's in the west wing?"

Lumière placed his hand behind his back as he replied, "Nothing, nothing. Storage space."

Ella looked at the clock and her replied nodding, "Storage space."

"Yes, that's it." Lumière exclaimed as he smiled at her nervously. Ella frowned but, let go of the matter as they walked further on.

"This way, please to the east wing." Mr. Cogsworth said as he led them to the east wing and Lumière corrected him, "And as I like to call it, the only wing."

As they reached the east wing, Lumière jumped down from Ella's hand as he stepped forward. He opened the door and said to her, "Welcome to your new home." Ella looked around nervously as she entered the room, only to have her breath taken away.

"Its modest, but comfortable." Lumière reasoned as he moved around in the room.

The room was decorated with paintings of intricate designs all over the walls and the furniture matched the golden aesthetic of the room. Ella looked at the blue, grey and green combinations of paint in the room paired with gold. The room was as big as the one in her home and she choked as she said, "It's..beautiful."

Ella stood in front of the mirror and stared at her reflection as she heard Lumière, "But, of course. Master wanted you to have the finest room in the castle." He jumped on the bed and the dust engulfed him as he coughed,

"Oh, dear. We were not expecting guests." Ella chuckled at him and was startled as a dove shaped Featherduster flew right past her. The Featherduster greeted her as she swept all the dust from the room, "Enchantè, mademoiselle. Don't worry. I'll have this place spotless in no time." She flew around the room gracefully and Ella's eyes followed her movements as she dusted the room.

Ella looked at the Featherduster as she saw her land on the bed and walk right into Lumière's arms. Featherduster caressed Lumière's cheek as she said, "This plan of yours is dangerous." Lumière tugged her closer as he said, "I would do anything to kiss you again, Plumette." Plumette the Featherduster shook her head as she said, "No, my love. I have been burnt before." He tugged her closer and they both stared into each other's eyes. Mr. Cogsworth cleared his throat and they broke apart, Ella chuckled lightly at them as she wandered in the room.

She walked towards the table and asked, "Is everything alive in here?" She picked up a hairbrush and turned it around as she observed, "Hello?" Lumière smacked his forehead as he replied clearing her doubts, "It's just a hairbrush."

Suddenly, the wardrobe next to Ella opened and she stumbled back as the wardrobe sang a high note. Lumière stepped down from the bed and stood next to Ella as he said, "Miss, meet Madame De Garderobe, the greatest singer of all time."

"Wish you can awake." Mr. Cogsworth mumbled slowly but, Madame Garderobe heard him as she replied, "Cogsworth. A diva needs a beauty rest." She didn't complete the sentence as she yawned loudly.

Lumière spoke loudly, "Madame, stay with us. As we have someone for you to dress."

Madame Garderobe gasped out loud as she held Ella with her handles and tugged her forward, "Ah! Finally, a woman!" She massaged Ella's face as she said, "Pretty eyes, proud face. A perfect canvas. Yes!" She exclaimed as she dug into her drawers, "I'll fins you something worthy of a princess."

Ella shook her head no as she reasoned, "I'm not a princess."

Madame Garderobe shook her head as she said, "Non sense! Let me see what I have got in my drawer." She said as she opened her drawers one by one and took out different pieces of clothing's. She held Ella in a place as she put the puffy underskirt on and then she kept on throwing random clothes onto make her dress.

Ella heard a dog's bark and she saw a footstool run into the room and Madame Garderobe called out, "Froufrou, come and help mama." The footstool stood near Ella as the clothes wrapped around her and twirled her around as she lost her balance and Froufrou held a piece of cloth in his mouth which he tightened by, tugging it down. Ella gasped as the corset around her tightened and she almost choked. Madame Garderobe placed a white wig on her head and exclaimed, "Perfecto!"

Ella saw as Lumière, Plumette and Mr. Cogsworth retreated slowly with their backs to the door and Lumière complimented Madame Garderobe, "Subtle, understated. I love it!" He bowed down as he walked out of the room and heard Madame Garderobe speak, "Froufrou, send my love to the maestro." The door closed as Froufrou ran out of the door and Madame Garderobe fell into a fit of snoring. Ella ducked down as she got out of the dress and crawled towards the windows. As she reached the windows, she stood up and looked down, calculating the distance in her head. She sighed as she realised it was mere impossible to climb down, but as her gaze fell on the heaps of clothes, she grinned as a "Perfecto!" idea formed in her head.

~~~

Beast

The Beast threw the vase on the floor in anger and it broke into pieces just like his heart. He had hoped that he would be able to turn into human again, as he had asked the Enchantress for two days. But, once he turned Beast again, it changed him more into a monster and he was angry as he had scared the girl. He was angry at everything, he was angry at the world, at the girl for getting scared, although it wasn't her fault. He wanted to be human again and live a normal life.

He groaned out loud as he smashed the wall mirror in his room and it shattered into pieces and one of the pieces cut his hand. He stared at the blood on his hands, as he realised that maybe he had hurt the girl same way, emotionally, when he had approached her the night before. The look in her eyes, matched the blood dripping out from his fingers, and he sighed out loud as he sat down near the broken pieces of glass. He growled out loud at the misery in his life and looked around the mess he had created in his room. His life looked the same and it was his fault. Every wrong thing in the world was his fault. He was at fault for ruining the lives of his servants. They were trapped in this haunting castle, because of him and he could never forgive himself for it.

The guilt would be trapped in his mind through his life.

The Enchantress had cursed him such as he would become the monster he had always feared. He was becoming like the monster in his nightmares more as the days passed and he could do nothing about him.

The fear in the girl's eyes reminded him of his childhood when he would wake up in the middle of the night, scared because of the nightmare, sweat dripping down his forehead as he stared at the terrifying night.

Beast shook his head as he stood up and thought of visiting the girl in the nursing room, to check up on her as she had blacked out due to his appearance. He hoped he wouldn't scare her away once again. He stepped down the stairs one by one as he strode to the nursing room. It was dead silent in the castle, as always whenever he walked out of his room and the hallway was lit dimly as he walked.

He neared the nursing room and he couldn't sense any movements from inside the room and he assumed she would still be asleep. So, he knocked lightly on the door waiting for her to wake up and open the door. He stood there for a few minutes before he knocked harder this time. Still, no response was heard from the insides as waited impatiently. He grew angry as he threw the door open and strode inside. He stomped his foot as he looked around the room, to find it empty.

He turned his head sideways as he searched every corner in the room. He picked up the heavy blanket from the blanket and found nothing. He walked to the open window and looked down to find any signs of the girl. There was no way she could have jumped out of here, he thought. He threw the wardrobe open and was met with nothing again. He lost his temper as he threw the furniture around and growled loudly at the empty room.

He strode out of the room, angrily as he thought of the places she could have hid in the castle. He searched the hallway to end up with no result. He growled loudly as he ended up in front of the staircase leading up to the wings. He looked around hurriedly, wanting to see the girl in front of him. He eyed the coat hanger warily as he stood straight not moving at all. He narrowed his eyes as he picked up him and asked, "Where is the girl?"

The coat hanger seemed frightened as he answered, "I...I.. don't know, Master. I don't know." This angered Beast even more as he tightened his grip around his neck and asked again, "I'm asking for the last time, where is the girl?" He roared at him and the coat hanger shook in his hands as he stuttered, "I don't know, Master. I saw Lumière talking about her few minutes ago. I don't know where she is." As he finished talking, Beast heard Lumière's voice coming from the west wing. He turned his head as he tried making sense of what Lumière was saying. He loosened his grip on the coat hanger's neck as he left him and made his way to the west wing.

He walked up the stairs and heard Lumière and Mr. Cogsworth speaking in the west wing. He growled out loud at the voices, "Lumière!" His voice silenced the castle, as he heard Lumière run towards him from the west wing. Lumière stopped to breathe as he bent down in front of his Master. Beast narrowed his eyes at Lumière and Mr. Cogsworth shrugged at him, lightly.

"Lumière! Where is the girl?" He asked him as he waited for the answer and Lumière stood up straight smiling at him. "Don't smile at me. Give me the answer, where is the girl?" Beast asked losing the last bit of patience he had in him.

Lumière smiled nervously at him as he scratched his neck and replied, "You see, Master. The girl..." The Beast nodded at him to continue, "The girl..." Lumière stopped and took his Master's hand in his and he walked them away from the west wing.

Beast was hesitant but, followed him nonetheless as Lumière was the only one knowing her whereabouts. "Where is the girl, Lumière?" The Beast asked as they reached his bedroom. Lumière closed the door behind him as Mrs. Potts soon followed soon and all of them were in the closed spacing. The room was dead silent as Beast waited for Lumière to answer his question. Lumière looked anywhere but him as he was nervous.

"The girl is in her room." Mrs. Potts uttered out of nowhere as everyone starred at her in disbelief. Beast was confused as he asked, "You gave her a room?" Mrs. Potts smiled at him and he scrunched his face in anger. "Why would you give her a room? She doesn't deserve to be in this castle as she's a nobody." Mrs. Potts narrowed her eyes at him as she asked, "Now, now. We don't have a right to judge anybody, do we?" Beast huffed at her as he was annoyed.

Lumière interrupted to lighten the mood, "It's okay, Master. She was scared that's all. She had never seen you in this form before, so…" Lumière looked down as Beast dared him to continue.

"She's a nice girl, Master." Lumière said as he scratched his head nervously. "Maybe you should ask her to have dinner with you as she's our guest." Beast scoffed at the word 'guest' and shook his head.

"Why should I ask her?" The Beast said and it was Mrs. Potts who broke the silence that followed, "Because, you have to. It's your duty." Beast shook his head once again but, as Mrs. Potts narrowed her eyes at him, he reluctantly agreed.

"Alright, fine. I'll ask her. But, how do I ask her?" Beast said as he paced in the room. Lumière smiled at him as he gestured his hand around wildly, "It's simple, Master. You knock on her door and ask 'Would you like to join me for dinner?'." Beast rolled his eyes at Lumière's suggestion but, nonetheless walked out of his bedroom, everyone following suit.

They reached her bedroom in the west wind and Beast stood in front of her door. He looked at them and shook his head at them but, one look from Mrs. Potts and he knocked on the door hesitantly.

"Yes." He heard a mumbled reply from behind the door and he ordered loudly, "Join me for dinner!" He heard a scoff from her and he growled lightly. "No, I won't have dinner with you. You first take me as your prisoner and then ask me to have dinner with you?"

He grew angry as he scratched the door with his claws and threw the furniture from the hallway around. The servants barely managed to save themselves as Mrs. Potts shouted at him, "Ask her nicely." Beast scoffed but, still asked her one more time.

"Would you like to join me for dinner?" He asked in a soft tone and waited impatiently for her answer. He heard a loud, "No!" from the bedroom and he strode away angrily while growling out loud at them and they took a step back in fear.

"If she doesn't eat with me, she doesn't eat atall." He said as he turned away from the room and stomped towards his room angrily.

~~~

Cinderella - I

Ella tugged the hair behind her ear, as it teased her cheek. She sighed as she looked at the room and saw clothes all over it. Madame Garderobe was still asleep as she did her work. Ella had managed to create a rope with the help of the clothes. She tightened the knot on the piece of cloth she was holding and as she held it in her hands, she heard a knock. She turned towards it confused and asked, "Yes?"

She heard a loud groan from outside as she heard Beast speak, "Join me for dinner!" She took a sharp intake of breath as she remembered the monster from last night and how hideous he looked. The sharp fangs of his and his monstrous size with the fur covering him. She gathered her strength as she yelled, "No! I won't have dinner with you. You first take me as your prisoner and then ask me to have dinner with you?" She said as she walked towards the door and heard a loud growl as the supposed Beast threw the furniture around in anger and all the servants around him, shrieked in fear.

She heard a lady's voice and she frowned as the lady shouted at the Beast, "Ask her nicely." Ella listened to the conversations going on the outside as she placed her ear on the door and strained to listen. She heard the Beast scoff loudly before he spoke again, "Would you like to join me for dinner?"

Ella sighed again as she calmed her heart before she yelled, "No!" She took a step back from the door as she heard a banging on the door and looked at the door frightening before the Beast growled, "If she doesn't eat with me, she doesn't eat at all." She sighed a breath of relief as she realised he won't barge in the room angrily.

She walked back to the window as she stared down and sighed. She won't be home soon, she realised. Her legs gave up as she remembered her house and how her evil stepmother and stepsisters would be treating it. She knew they didn't care about the house and she had to go back to take care of the house. It was her Papa's and Mama's last belonging and she wanted to cherish it as much as she could. She was ready to live as a servant for her evil stepmother if it meant living in the attic of her house.

She looked down as she cherished the moments she lived in her house and not some monster's. She wanted to be back in the warmth of her house, the chirpiness of the animals and the beauty of her house. She clenched her knees as tears fell down and she hugged herself. She cried for a second before she realised, she had to be strong and have courage. Her mother had taught her to do so. She quickly wiped her tear stained cheeks as she stood up and picked up the rope of clothes she had made. She calculated the distance between the window and the ground.

Ella measured the ropes and decided she had to add more clothes. She picked up the remaining clothes from the floor and started tying them in knots.

~~~

Lumière warmed himself in front of the fire as he heard the stones falling from the walls and he sighed as he spoke, "Another petal fell." He sighed as he looked down at his body and saw his legs become more metallic. He turned around as he heard Plumette call him, "Lumière, I grew three more feathers." She said as she caressed her feathers. Plumette sat on the chair in front of the fire and warmed herself, "And I just plugged yesterday."

Lumière walked towards her as he reassured her, "I know, darling." He said as he straightened his leg, "I'm getting more metallic every day." He kicked his leg in the air and it seemed to relieve him some of the pain he was having.

They heard Mr. Cogsworth groan again as the clock hands moved in circle and he seemed puzzled, "Oh no, it's happening again." He said as his blinked trying to stable himself, "Pardon me." He apologised as the gears in his body tightened.

Mrs. Potts spoke loudly as she sat on the table, "Oh, everyone calm yourselves. We still have time." She shook her head as she turned to Chip who called out to her, "Mama," Chip said as he jumped towards her and stood next to her, "Am I ever going to be a boy again?"

Mrs. Potts gushed as she tugged Chip closer to her, "Oh, yes, Chip. You will have your days in the Sun again." She hugged him tightly and placed a kiss on his edge as she spoke, "You just leave it to me."

~~~

Ella smiled lightly as she stared at the long rope of clothes she had made and threw one end of it down from the window. She had tied the second end of the rope to the legs of bed. She straightened the ropes as she heard a knock on the door. She turned around hastily as she yelled, "I told you to go away." She looked at the door, waiting for it to be busted open by the Beast but she was greeted by the lovely voice of the lady from earlier, "Oh, honey, it's me Mrs. Potts. Don't worry, dear."

Ella quickly hid the remaining ends of the rope behind her legs as she stood in front of it and waited for Mrs. Potts to enter the room. She stood nervous as the door to her room opened and in strode a table, along with a Tea Pot and a tea cup on it. The Tea Pot spoke, "Oh, aren't you a vision.

How lovely of me to be of your acquaintance! I'm Mrs. Potts." Mrs. Potts walked further into the room and looked at the rope made by Ella. She smiled at her lightly as Ella tried to hide her plans.

Mrs. Potts looked up at her as she spoke, "It's a very long journey dear. Let me fix you up before you go." Ella looked at her suspiciously before she looked at the rope hanging from the windows.

Mrs. Potts stopped in the centre of the room, "I have found, that most of the troubles seems less troubling, after a bracing cup of tea." Mrs. Potts said calmly as she poured a cup of tea for Ella in the tea cup. "Slowly now, Chip." She said to Chip who bounced in his place. Mrs. Potts reminded Ella of her grandmother as she was just as sweet. Ella walked towards her as she smiled lightly, she trusted her for some reason and picked up the tea cup from the table.

Ella took a sip from the tea and warmth filled her up as she smiled. She held the saucer in her hand and she saw as the tea cup turned around. The cup had eyes and lips as she smiled at her, "Hello, I'm Chip! Pleased to meet you." Ella chuckled lightly at his enthusiasm as she took in his appearance. "Wanna see me do a trick?" He asked as he didn't wait for Ella's answer and made a bubble from the tea and popped it. "Chip!" Mrs. Potts exclaimed at her child but, Ella didn't mind him one bit as she smiled at him. He reminded her of Gus and Jaq. Ella smiled sadly as she remembered them.

"It was a very brave of you, my dear to stand your ground." Mrs. Potts said as Madame Garderobe woke up and opened the doors of her closer as she spoke, "Yes, we all think so."

Ella smiled at them sadly as she said, "My Mama taught me to always be kind and have courage." Mrs. Potts smiled at her as she said, "That's a quite lovely, dear. Your mother sounds wise. How is she? Do you miss her?" A tear fell down Ella's cheeks and she wiped it quickly as she said, "She's no more." Mrs. Potts looked down sadly as she spoke, "I'm sorry, dear." Ella shook her head, "It's alright. I do miss her a lot."

"Cheer up, my puppet." Mrs, Potts said as Ella walked towards her, "Things will turn out in the end. You'll feel lot better after dinner." She said as she nodded towards the door.

Ella was confused as she looked at Mrs. Potts and asked, "But, 'If she doesn't eat with me, she doesn't eat at all.'" She questioned Mrs. Potts as she scrunched her eyebrows together. Mrs. Potts chuckled at her as she said, "People say a lot of things in anger. It is our choice whether or not to listen." She made her way to the door and turned towards Ella as she asked, "You coming, puppet?"

Ella looked at Madame Garderobe as she mumbled, "Go!" Ella sighed lightly as she rushed towards Mrs. Potts and walked out of the room together.

~~~

A/N : Here's a cute little pic of Chip, cause you guys are the best xD

Cinderella - II

"They are coming!" Lumière shouted as he and Mr. Cogsworth rushed into the kitchen. "Final checks, everyone!" Lumière clasped his hands together as he looked around in the hustling kitchen. He climbed the dishwasher as Mr. Cogsworth tried running towards him but failed to do so and huffed out a breath as he looked at Lumière, "No, you don't! Do you realise how furious Master will be after he finds out about your plan? He will blame it all on me."

Lumière shrugged at him as he said looking at the washed plates on the rack, "Yes, I'll make sure of it." He picked up a plate as he handed it to the coat hanger to dry off and he said, "But, did you see her stand up to him? I'm telling you, this girl is the one." He picked up a spoon and handed it to the coat hanger and said, "Hey, chauffer, you missed a spot." He jumped off from the dishwasher and landed on the table. "You know; she'll never love him." Mr. Cogsworth said as he looked at Lumière.

Mr. Cogsworth climbed slowly on the moving table and Lumière helped him up as he said, "A broken clock is right two times a day, but this is not one of those time, Cogsworth. Stand up straight." Lumière said as he moved onto the fireplace as he exclaimed, "It's time to sparkle!" He looked at the utensils cooking the food and he encouraged them as he spoke, "I have no taste buds but, I can tell it's going to taste amazing."

The cook who had been turned into stove muttered annoyingly, "Get off me while I work!" Lumière checked as he looked into the utensils, "Pepper! Salt!" Mr. Cogsworth scoffed at his enthusiasm as she scolded Lumière, "Not so loud, keep it down!" Lumière sighed as he said, "Of course, of course. But, what is a dinner without a little music?" He cleaned the candle stand on the table with a cloth and placed it down nicely as he jumped down from the table and made his way out of the room. Mr. Cogswoth scoffed as he followed Lumière, "Music?"

Lumière spotted Maestro Cadanza and rushed towards him, "Maestro Cadanza, are you ready?" He asked at the old piano and the old, rusty piano sighed at him as he answered, "It has been so long since I've performed." The piano walked slowly towards Lumière and he played his keys lightly as he muttered, "I can't barely even remember how." Maestro Cadanza began playing the keys and it started out nice as he played a tune but, as he reached a higher note, the keys stopped with a loud shriek, causing Maestro Cadanza to groan out loud.

"Another cavity." Maestro Cadanza sighed as he looked down at his keys. Lumière looked up at him sadly as he spoke, "Maestro, your wife is upstairs. Finding it harder and harder to stay awake." Lumière walked closer to him as he spoke, "She's counting on you to help us break this curse." Maestro Cadanza straightened up as he proudly looked at Lumière, "Then, I shall play through the dental pain."

Mr. Cogsworth stood next to Lumière and he asked Maestro Cadanza, "Maestro, can you play quartet, please?" Maestro Cadanza scoffed at him as he sarcastically muttered, "Oh, quartet. Of course!" He looked at narrowing his eyes and asked, "Are there any other tasteless demands you wished to make upon my artistry?"

Mr. Cogsworth didn't get the memo as he innocently replied, "No, that's it." All three of them heard footsteps approaching them. Mrs. Potts spoke loudly, "There you go darling!"

Lumière showed Ella the way as they entered the dining room. The room was dark as she walked in and saw Plumette fly in the air and hold a mirror in her hand as it reflected the light on the table. Lumière followed the light's reflection and stood in it as he welcomed Ella, "Mademoiselle!" He held his hands behind his back as he greeted her, "It is with the deepest pride and greatest pleasure that we welcome you tonight." He took a step forward as he spoke, "And now, we invite you to relax." He said as bowed in front of her.

Ella gasped as she was pushed to sit down as a chair appeared and her knees gave in. "Let us pull up a chair!" She heard Lumière speak as she glanced back at him. She smiled lightly at him as he continued, "As the dining room proudly presents-" He smiled at her and as he gestured his hands in the air, the dishes and the cutlery all flew in the air and settled themselves in front of her. The music playing in the background suddenly stopped and Lumière looked at Maestro Cadanza nervously, but Maestro Cadanza managed to end the note and Lumière finished, "Your dinner!"

Silence filled the room as Ella stared at Lumière in surprise. She saw him get up as he sang, "Be our Guest!" He stood up slowly as he looked at her, "Be our Guests! Tie your napkin around your neck, cheer up. And we'll provide the rest!" Lumière sang as he twirled around himself and Ella awed in surprise as saw the dining room lit up in colours. The coat hanger around her tied a napkin around her neck and Ella smiled at him.

"Go on, unfold your menu!" Lumière said as Ella was handed a menu by Plumette, she thanked her as she opened the menu. "Take a glance and then you'll be our guest. Be our Guest!" Lumière sang graciously as all the dishes danced around him.

Ella smiled as she picked up the wine glass placed in front of her and Lumière sang as he danced around the table. The cutlery following his steps as he entertained her. "We'll prepare the food and serve with flair a culinary cabaret." He sang as all the glasses mimicked his step and Ella chuckled at his silly moves.

"You're alone and you're scared but, the banquet's all prepared." Ella took a sip of the red wine and saw as the cutlery stood along the tables and Lumière walked towards them, "No one's gloomy or complaining while the flatware's entertaining." He jumped on the napkin held by the forks as he exclaimed, "We tell jokes, I do tricks with my fellow candle sticks." He swung in the air as he held onto the chandelier and the chandelier turned around as he hung on it and waved his hand around.

Ella heard the rest of the servants singing in chorus and smiled at their goofiness, "And it's all in perfect taste that you can bet." Lumière jumped down from the chandelier as he continued, "Come on and lift your glass. You've won your on free pass to be our guest." Lumière sang as he stood up and all the servants stood in the final position before her. "Be our Guest!" They all ended the song and Lumière rushed to her as he held a plate in his hands and asked her, "Puding?" and bowed down as they finished their performance.

Ella chuckled at him as she took the plate out of his hands and set it on the table as she thanked him.

~~~

Ella walked next to Mrs. Potts as they made their way towards the staircase. She turned to her and asked, "I don't understand why you all are being kind to me?"

She shook her head as she walked, "Surely, you're as trapped here as I am. Don't you ever want to escape?" She asked Mrs. Potts. Mrs. Potts turned to her as she replied chuckling lightly, "The Master is not as terrible as he appears. Somewhere deep in his soul, there's still a prince.." Mrs. Potts stopped as Ella's face scrunched in confusion and she struggled to place her words as she continued, "Of a fellow just waiting to be set free." Ella nodded at Mrs. Potts as she finished and turned towards the staircase leading up to the west wing. As she looked at the wings, she asked Mrs. Potts, "Lumière mentioned something about the west wing." Ella narrowed her eyes as she looked at the wing but, turned her head as she heard Mrs. Potts speak, "Never you mind about that. Off to bed with you puppet." Mrs. Potts nodded as she took her leave and went her way.

Ella nodded at her and walked up the stairs leading up to the west wing. She climbed the stairs slowly as she waited for Mrs. Potts to turn around the corner. As she saw, Mrs. Potts go on her way, Ella fastened her pace as she climbed two steps at a time and made her way to the stairs leading to the west wing.

The curiosity took the best of her as she ventured into the dark wing. The aura around her seemed dark and the air was cold. Ella shivered as she climbed the stairs. The sound of her footsteps echoing in the dark silence that followed in the castle. Ella looked back as she feared that someone might catch her but, nonetheless her foots took her forward. She glanced at the high walls and the dark curtains that covered them in a demeanour.

Ella saw a huge closed door in front of her and she rushed towards it. She held the handle to the doors in her hand and she pushed them open as she entered the room. The door shut behind her with a loud thud as she entered the hideous looking room. She glanced around as she saw the room dimly lit with torches. She walked inside as she saw a huge painting on the wall in front of her. She stopped in front of the painting as she observed it. The painting was of a woman, a child and a man. The painting was torn from down below and the man's face was scratched off. She saw the woman's eyes and she felt like she had seen them somewhere before. She scrunched her face in confusion as she moved further into the room.

She saw a huge mess of things fallen down on the floor as a table was broken in front of her and the curtains were pulled down. She ignored the mess as she turned left to the king size bed in front of her. As she turned left, she saw a balcony leading out of the room. She walked closer to it and realized that the wind was getting colder. The balcony was covered in snow as cold wind blew. There was a table set in the middle of the balcony. The demeanor of the balcony was dark and cold, shivers covering Ella's body. She hugged herself as she tried getting used to the cold.

Ella reached the table and saw a rose was kept on the table, with a glass lid keeping it covered. There were petals around the rose, which had fallen it seemed. Ella bent her head down as she looked at it. She saw it sparkle a little and it suddenly took her back to the night when she had met her fairy godmother. The fairy godmother's magical wand sparkled the same way and Ella took a step back in shock.

But, as she looked at the rose, the petals around it were burned and only few were remaining. It was just a mere coincidence, she thought, remembering her fairy godmother. She glanced at the rose and rose her hand to touch the glass covering the rose. As she touched the glass, she heard a loud thud from her left. She took a step back as she was startled by the sound. She saw as Beast neared with an angry stance and pushed her away from the rose as he caressed the glass covering the rose, checking for any damages.

He turned to look at her with rage in his eyes as he asked, "What did you do to it?"

~~~

Beast

The Beast was furious as he left the servants at the girl's door, as she refused to eat with him. He strode out of the wing and headed towards his study as he couldn't bear to be in the same environment as her. She was infuriating as she refused his request, given that he had forced her but, it was still a rude thing to do. She was the sweetest person he had met other than his mother, and he didn't want to hurt her but he ended up being on her hatred end.

Beast reached his study as he strode in and sat on the chair in front of him. He looked around the papers spread in front of him, they were laying there since years and he couldn't get himself to look at them. There al belonged to the royal work as he was supposed to do when he would be ruling around the Village but, he had failed his mother who had taught him the little things in life. He was furious at him for not changing, his father for being cruel and at his mother for being the sweet understanding person she was.

As he thought of his mother, he found courage and finally picked up the papers after years and stared at them as he read the papers. The papers were about the taxations and he was making a plan to raise the taxes before everything that happened. He supposed what happened to him were the consequences of his cruel system and his selfishness. But, he couldn't help himself as he was just a mere teenager when the Enchantress had cursed him. He was given full custody of the gold in the castle and all he wanted to do was spend them over luxuries. He was doing that, but soon he discovered that gold can finish too and you had to earn them more to spend. But, he was taught he was a prince and he wasn't supposed to earn them, he could steal them from the villagers by taxing them. And thus, he proceeded to do the same.

He never knew the concept of earning gold; he knew only to spend it. He kept on increasing the taxes around the Village and the villagers complied as they had no choice but, to do so. He secured the Village from the Outsiders and they gave him gold. He threw lavish parties and drank alcohol as he bathed in luxuries.

The Beast was broken from his memory as he heard Mr. Cogsworth loud voice scolding Lumière over something. He looked out through his study's door and tried making sense of the voices. He gave up a second later as he couldn't for the life of him get up and see what they were up to. Instead, he looked down at the papers in his hands, and picked up a pen in his hands, the claws making the paper seem fragile in his hand.

The feeling of holding the pen in his hand was foreign to him after all these years and he shrugged his hands once, trying to get the sense back. He shook his head as he put the paper down on the table and held the pen in his hand. He scratched out the old value of tax and lessened the percentage ten times as he wrote a new value on the paper. He smiled lightly as he had done something progressive since his change. He smiled sadly remembering his mother, but the image in front of his eyes was replaced by the girl from earlier. The way her eyes were widened as she stared at him. He shook his head as he closed his eyes, trying to forget that image.

Suddenly, something in his heart tugged as his heart constricted. He knew what was wrong as he ran towards his bedroom. He feared something had happened to the rose. He climbed the walls leading to the balcony with his claws, as it was a shorter way than climbing the stairs. As he neared the balcony, he saw the girl standing next to the rose. She touched the glass lid covering the rose and his heart burned.

His eyes widened as rage filled his mind as quickly jumped down on the balcony with a loud thud. The girl turned her head towards him and her eyes widened as she took him in. He quickly walked over to the rose and pushed the girl aside as she saw the rose sparkle in the dim light. Something is wrong, he thought. The Beast had never seen the rose sparkle like this before. He touched the glass trying to find any scratches but found nothing. He turned his head to look at the girl who was standing few steps away from him, clutching her wrist in her hand as she caressed it. He asked her as he saw nothing but rage, "What are you doing here? What did you do to it?"

The girl was scared as she answered, "Nothing." She looked at him with fera in her eyes and that cause to anger him more as he asked her, taking a step towards her, "Do you realise what you could have done? You could have ruined us all." He stomped his foot heavily as he walked towards her. He growled at her as he neared here, "Go!" He roared out loud as he pushed her away, and the girl ran away from him as he turned back to check the rose.

He closed the doors of his bedroom shut, not wanting to let anyone near the rose. He had to keep it safe at all cost. He walked over to the balcony as he looked down. He saw the girl getting on the horse. She quickly sat on it and rushed out of the gates. He saw her ride out of the gateway and sighed in relief as she entered the forest. The night was dark and a few seconds later, he heard the howling of the wolves. His eyes widened as he heard the loud neighing of the horse.

~~~

Cinderella

A/N : If you want to, you can listen to Wolves by Selena Gomez ft. Marshmellow. Cause, its an amazing song and it suits the scenery perfectly xD

~~~

Ella's eyes widened as she stared at the angry Beast. It was the first time; she had seen him after the night. She calmed herself as she tried not to faint as she answered his question with, "Nothing." She stumbled back as he pushed her back from the rose and looked at it to check any broke any pieces. She took in the scene in front of her as she saw the Beast caress the glass lid and he turned towards her as he screamed, "Do you realise what you could have done? You could have ruined us all." Ella took steps back as he walked towards her, he stomped his foot angrily on the floor and Ella's heart raced at the sound. She was frightened to death, as she stared at the creature in front of her. He roared out a loud, "Go!" This broke her from her stance as Ella turned around and ran like her life depended on it out of the room. She left the door thud behind her and she heard him close the door shut. But, she didn't stop as she rushed down the stairs.

She didn't want to be in this castle any longer and as she reached the stairs leading to the main door, she saw Lumière and Mr. Cogsworth in the foyer playing chess. She paid them no mind as she rushed down. She heard Lumière call her out, "Mademoiselle, where are you going?" They threw the chess board as they rushed after her and she heard Mrs. Potts shout loudly, "Where are you going?"

Ella was out of breath as she replied, "I'm leaving. I don't want to stay here any longer." Ella saw Mrs. Potts in her peripheral vision as she looked at the main door. Mrs. Potts yelled, "Don't let her leave." The coat hanger in front of the main gate, closed the door and locked it. Madame Garderobe walked out of the east wing because of the shouting, as she saw Ella was trying to leave she ordered Froufrou, "Go, Froufrou stop her." The footstool jumped down the stairs and stood in front of Ella who had now reached the end of the stairs. He stood on his legs and he licked Ella's hand and urged him to play with her.

"Not no, Froufrou. No play." Lumière sighed as he smacked his forehead. Ella nodded her head at the footstool and he ran towards the door. He opened the small adjoin door in the main door and ran outside. Lumière smacked his head again as the footstool had made Ella's escape easy. Ella didn't wait for anything as she ran towards the main door and made her way out through the small door.

As she stepped outside, she was hit with a wave of cold wind as the snow fell down. The entrance was filled with snow and Ella walked through the thick snow. She saw a horse outside the castle and she ran towards it. She saddled him and quickly climbed on him. She tugged on the ropes as she balanced herself. She bent down on the horse as she kicked him forward.

The cold air of the night hit her in the face as she rode towards the entrance. She didn't glance back once as she rode out. She rode through the gardens and fastened her speed as she saw the entrance. As she left the castle back, she sighed and rode into the forest. The forest was silent as a cemetery and Ella feared a little as she made her way through the forest.

A moment had passed and Ella was deep in the forest, she looked up at the moon and saw it shining brightly amongst the fog. She looked ahead as she saw a tree in the middle of the path. She heard the loud howling of the wolves and her eyes widened with realisation and she quickened her pace. She looked around her and saw some movements from her left. She turned around to look back and she gasped as she saw a pack of wolves chasing her. She looked ahead quickly and the horse neighed loudly as she saw a wolf in front of her. She gripped the ropes tighter as the horse jumped.

The horse moved in places as she saw the deadly fangs of the wolves and her heart beat loudly. She saw as a wolf jumped on the horse and she quickly slid down from the horse and picked up a log of wood she found on the ground. She turned around swiftly as she saw the wolves corner her. A wolf jumped towards her and she swung the log of wood at him. She missed him and the wolf landed next to her. She walked away from him as another wolf ran towards her, he barely managed to hit him but, she saved herself.

Ella stopped in her tracks as she heard a growl coming from behind her and she turned around to find a wolf on the top of small snow hill. She saw as she growled at her and fangs of his. Her eyes widened as she knew she couldn't survive him, as he was the same size as hers. The wolf took a step back as he readied himself and jumped at Ella, Ella put her hand up in defence and readied herself for the attack and closed her eyes. But, the attack never came.

As she opened her eyes, Ella saw the Beast jump on the wolf and take him down. He put his whole weight on the wolf and he covered the wolf's face with his claws. He growled as the wolf bit hit in his paw. She saw as the beast scratched the wolf's stomach with his claw. The wolf cried out in pain as he bit the Beast in defence.

Ella shuddered as another wolf jumped on the Beast's back. She saw as the Beast pried the wolf away by catching him by his neck and throwing away. The wolf hit the tree and fell down as he cried in pain. The wolf which the Beast had been fighting, had managed to pin the Beast down and climb on him as he bit him one more time. Another wolf held the Beast's leg in his mouth as the Beast struggled with the wolf on top of him.

The Beast groaned loudly as he kicked off the wolf trying to bite him in the leg and pushed the wolf on top of him to the ground. He stood up as looked at her but, just then another wolf jumped on his back and the Beast growled out loud as he got a hold of the wolf and threw him on the ground. The wolf hit the ground with a loud thump as he fell down. The wolf whimpered in pain as he stood up but, before he could try to fight again; the Beast got down on his hands as he roared out loud at them and his fangs shines brightly in the moon light. Ella was frozen in her spot as she saw the Beast transform into a real Beast and growl at them.

The wolves ran away from them as they saw the Beast, silence following suit behind them. The Beast stood up as he stared at Ella, her eyes following his movement. She shuddered as the Beast's legs gave up and he fell down on the snow with thud. She turned towards her horse as she remembered how he had shouted at her, and she caressed the horse; saddling him. Ella looked up at the glowing moon and it reminded her of the rose in his balcony. She heard the whimpers from the Beast and reluctantly she turned around to face him.

She sighed as she took in his injured self, she couldn't help herself as she removed the coat from her horse and opened it before she spread it on the lying Beast. The Beast opened his eyes slowly as he looked at her through pain. She smiled at him sadly as she said, "You have to help me." The Beast looked at her confused as she nodded at him, "You have to stand up." She said to him as she helped him stand up. She helped him walk towards the horse and made him sit on it. She tightened the coat around him as she turned the horse with the help of the ropes and made her way back to the castle. The beast was whimpering in pain as they slowly walked through the thick snow. Ella sighed to herself as she saw his wound on his claw. The fur on his claw had been ripped from the wolf's bite and Ella felt bad for him.

She looked ahead as the moonlight lit the path for them.

~~~

Cinderella

The Beast growled out at Ella's touch and she retrieved her hand, "That hurts!" The Beast roared at her as she tried to apply medicine to his wounded area on his arm. Ella scrunched her face in anger as she replied, "If you held still, it wouldn't hurt as much." The Beast scowled at her as he spoke, "If you hadn't run away, none of this would've happened." Ella's eyes widened as she stared at him in disbelief, "If you hadn't frightened me, I wouldn't have run away!"

The Beast scoffed at her reply as he looked at her, "Well, you shouldn't have been in the west wing!" Ella scowled as she spoke, "Well, you should learn to control your temper." The Beast huffed in anger as he turned around in his bed and faced the wall. Ella's scowl deepened as she saw his childishness. Her face scrunched up at the wound on his back as she tried to touch it, but retrieved her hand as she knew it would hurt him. She stood up from his bed as she spoke, "Try to get some rest."

She walked towards the door as she heard Mrs. Potts speak, "Thank you, miss." She stopped in front of them as Lumière bowed down in front of her, "We are eternally grateful." The Beast had fallen asleep as she looked back at him. She placed the cloth on the table and asked them, "Why do you care about him so much?"

Mrs. Potts, Mr. Cogsworth stood on the table as Mrs. Potts replied, "We have looked after him all his life." Ella tried making sense of thigs as she said, "But, he's cursed you somehow. Why?" She shrugged at them as she asked, "You have done nothing."

Mrs. Potts nodded at her as she spoke, "You're quite right there, dear." Mrs. Potts's expressions saddened as she looked at her, "You see, when the Master lost his mother and his cruel father took that sweet innocent lad, and twisted him to be just like him. We did nothing." She shook her head in shame and Ella turned to look at him and her heart broke at his self.

Lumière turned around as he motioned everyone to move out of the room, "Let him sleep." Ella left the room reluctantly as her heart constricted.

~~~

Ella walked back to her room as she thought of the love and hope that was still present in the castle even though there was so much sorrow. She reached the end of her hallway and entered the room, she looked at the snoring Madame Garderobe and her heart broke at the amount of pain all these living beings had to endure because of one cruel human being. The Beast's father reminded her of her own evil stepmother but, even though Lady Tremaine treated Ella this way she never treated her own daughters so badly. How twisted can a person be if they treated their own child this way? she thought as she stared out the window.

She had discovered that a person could be crueller than she had witnessed in her life and she knew she had to be more grateful of how the things were for her. She became wise and stronger than she ever was as she decided to help them out. She went to bed with a new purpose in her mind, even though she wasn't free from the castle.

The next morning as the sun shined brightly, Ella woke up and freshened herself as she and the servants made their way to the Beast's bedroom. She smiled at them and greeted them, "Good morning!" with a cheerful voice and they entered the bedroom to find Beast still asleep. She strode over to his bed and leaned on his bed to check his body temperature. She touched his forehead and found his body temperature had gone back to normal. She sighed in delight as she told the others the good news and sat at the couch, waiting for him to wake up. She leaned in front of the servants standing in front of her as she asked, "I want to help you out. What can I do?"

The servants looked baffled as they stared at her and then Mr. Cogsworth stepped towards her as he started, "Well, there's one way to help." Lumière pulled Mr. Cogsworth back by his arm as he smiled at her nervously. Ella looked at them confusingly as Mrs. Potts answered her question, "Dear, you needn't worry about that." Ella looked at her to continue, "We made our bed and we must lie in it." Ella frowned as she stared at her and then her gaze fell upon the rose in the balcony and she looked at it.

She turned towards them as she asked, "What happens when the last petal falls?" Lumière gestured at her as he spoke, "The Master remains a beast forever. And we become.." Mrs. Potts finishes his sentence as she says, "Antiques."

"Knick Knacks." Lumière relied shrugging.

"Lightly used houseware." Plumette replied flying around them

Mr. Cogsworth stepped forward as he spat out, "Rubbish."

"We become rubbish."

Ella sighed as she looked at the rose and saw another petal fall down and burn to ash.

~~~

"Love can transpose to form and dignity." Ella sat next to the Beast's bed as she spoke her favourite quotes and combed through her hair. She absentmindedly looked ahead, unaware as the Beast stirred in his sleep at her beautiful voice and didn't stop her as she continued reciting, "Love looks not with the eyes, but with the mind."

The Beast turned towards her as she looked at her and interrupted, "And, therefore is winged Cupid painted blind." He finished for her and gasped as she turned towards him. He sat up slowly in his bed as he groaned a little at the pain.

"You know Shakespeare?" Ella asked as she looked at him. The Beast held his hand as he replied, "I had an expensive education."

"Actually, Romeo and Juliet is my favourite play." Ella replied as she shrugged at him. The Beast huffed in annoyance as he fell back into the bed, "Ugh, why is that not a surprise?" He asked out loud. Ella seemed startled at his actions and she blinked in surprise as she asked him, "I'm sorry?"

The Beast tugged on his blanket as he answered her question, "Well, you know that heartache," He scrunched his face as he continued, "Pining, and blah,,blahh" He replied as he made weird vomiting faces at the love related words. Ella gaped at him as she saw his expressions.

"So many better things to read." He muttered finally as he was done with the vomiting expressions. Ella chuckled at him as she asked, "Like what?" She stared at him in disbelief.

The Beast stood up from the bed and freshened up as Ella waited for him to get ready. After he was done, they walked out of his bedroom and made their way towards a hallway to their right. As they reached the end of the hallway, the Beast opened up a door leading to a room. He walked inside and Ella followed suit.

"Well, there are a couple of things in here, which you could start." The Beast said as he walked towards a book shelf."

Ella entered the room and halted in her steps as she stared at the long, high shelfs covering the walls of the room and books stalked up in them. Her eyes widened as she saw the books in the room. He had his own library, and she struggled to find a good book to read. It was as if her dream had come true as everywhere she looked she saw heaps of books. She struggled to speak when he asked her, "You alright?" She turned towards him as her face lit up with so many emotions, she was overwhelmed with happiness and excitement as she replied, "Its wonderful!"

The Beast looked around in the library as he realised the beauty of the library, "Yes, I suppose it is." He saw as Ella looked around the library with a gleam in her eyes and he smiled at her as she turned to look at him.

He shrugged at her as he started, "Well, if you like it so much, then it's yours." He nodded at her as she smiled at him with a confused expression. He turned around as he walked towards a shelf. He heard her speak, "Have you read every one of these books?" He turned around as he saw her standing with her arms folded.

"What?" He asked her as the question confused him but, then he shrugged at her as he replied, "Well, not all of them." He scoffed at her question playfully as he spoke, "Some of them are in Greek."

Ella chuckled at him as she asked him, "Was that a joke?" She looked at him with a funny expression as she asked him, "Are you making jokes now?" The Beast looked at her nervously as he slowly nodded his head at her and looked anywhere but her as he replied, "Maybe." He shrugged as he walked towards the book shelf and Ella chuckled at his childishness.

~~~

"Floraison de l'amour"

Third POV

Ella chuckled loudly as she stared at the books and piles of book in the library. She couldn't believe her eyes as she took in the amount of books. They both sat at the library as they read the books, Beast had piled on the table. He looked her as she concentrated on reading the book. Her brows were furrowed as she read a certain sentence and the Beast smiled at her curious self. He had never seen someone who was this excited to read new books. Sure, he himself was an avid reader but, most people didn't like reading books. They preferred the live action plays. But, the Beast felt that the little things about the books couldn't be told through the plays, as those details could only be imagined through one's imagination. She looked beautiful reading the book, the Beast thought.

Ella smiled at something she read and she felt eyes on her as she turned the page. She looked at the Beast who was staring at from the corner of her eyes and as he realised that she knew he was staring, the Beast coughed a little as he turned towards his own book and pretended to be engrossed in it. Ella shook her head at him and continued reading pretending to not notice. He smiled at her lightly as he blushed.

The next day started out the same as Ella checked his wounds and applied medicines on them and the Beast gave her a new book to read as she managed to finish one in a day. Madame Garderobe had made new dresses for her to wear and they suited her way as she styled them according to her senses. Ella's so far dress was a red one, she wore today, it had a mini coat and it had a caped, it was thick with fur and kept her warm in the cold. Ella's eyes concentrated on the book she was reading as looked up to glance at the Beast. She was curious about him as he wasn't what she had imagined him to be. He had a soft heart and was good by nature.

They both sat at the dinner table at lunch time as they both had book stands in front of them along with the dishes. They sat at the ends of the table and the Beast looked at her as she drank her soup with the spoon as she read the book. His bowl was placed in front of him, he nervously glanced at her before he dipped his head down and drank the soup directly from the bowl. The soup covered his beard as he looked up and he swallowed. He knew that she saw him eat like an animal but, she pretended she didn't and continued reading her book as if nothing happened. He looked sideways as he smiled nervously. She chuckled at him lightly.

~~~

"The air is blue, keen and cold..." Ella spoke as they climbed the bridge in the garden, "and in a frozen sheath enrolled. Each branch, each twig.." Ella stopped as she saw the Beast turn sideways as he saw the frozen river beneath the bridge. The Beast took a sharp breath as he stared at the beauty of snow and water crystals. The reflection from the sky made it all much beautiful. He walked closer to the edge of the bridge and placed his hands on it as looked around the beauty. "each blade of grass, seems clad miraculously with..." Ella stopped reading as she looked at Beast and waited for him to speak. "...glass." She finished when she realised that he was waiting for her to finish.

She walked towards him and stood beside him taking in the beauty of the nature and heard him speak," Why does it feel like I'm seeing for the first time?" She was stunned at his question as she too realised that she felt like she had a rebirth. It was too beautiful to be described as the scenery in the front of them, was astounding.

Ella smiled at him as she stared at the awe expression on his face and Beast blushed at her stare. He shrugged at her as he struggled to put words together but, somehow he managed as he asked, "Is there anymore?" Ella's smiled widened as she looked at him but, as she saw him stare at her she looked down quickly into her book and fumbled with the pages as she turned them around and quickly nodded at him, "Yes, yes." She said out of breath as the Beast waited for her to read.

She chuckled lightly as she looked down and read, "But, in that solemn silence is heard the whisper of every sleeping thing." She looked at him as she saw him stare at the scenery and she continued looking down, "Look. Look at me." Beast's eyes widened as the realisation dawned on him and he turned to look at her as she continued, "Come wake me up for, still here I'll be." Ella looked up at him as she finished reading and blushed a little as she saw him staring at her and the Beast smiled at her lightly. They both looked ahead immediately breaking the gaze as they realised that they had been looking at each other adoringly.

~~~

Ella and the Beast walked next to each other as they walked towards the horse in front of the main door. The horse looked at them as they neared him and neighed and danced in his place as he saw the Beast in the broad day light. Ella rushed towards him as she held him in place as she griped the ropes in her hands. The Beast looked at her in wonder as he saw her coo into the horse's ears and calm him down by caressing his neck. Ella caressed the horse till he calmed down and smiled at him as he started breathing normally.

The Beast stood at a distance as he didn't wish to frighten the horse anymore. He himself was scared but, he strode towards the horse when Ella nodded at him. She slowly took his hand in hers and as the horse faced the other way, she placed it on his back. The Beast's eyes widened in awe as he felt the breathing of the horse and he turned to look at Ella who nodded at him and removed her hand from his. She walked away slowly as she smiled at him and started singing as she tugged the cape around her head, "There's something sweet and almost kind. But, he was mean and he was coarse and unrefined and now he's dear and so unsure, I wonder why I didn't see it there before." Ella climbed up the bridge as she saw the Beast caress the horse slowly and lightly, not to frighten him. He was so engrossed in it, that he didn't expect a snow ball fly towards him and hit him in the shoulder. Ella chuckled at his reaction as he was startled and looked around to find the source of the snow ball. As he turned his head, he saw Ella chuckling at his expense.

He smiled lightly as he bent down to make a snow ball of his and he hid it away from her. As he finished making it, he stood up and straight and threw it at Ella. Ella was so busy laughing at him that she didn't see the big snow ball coming at her and didn't duck in time as it hit her square in the face and she fell down due to its force. The Beast chuckled lightly at her as he scratched his neck nervously and looked down smiling to himself.

~~~

As they sat at the dinner table that night, the Beast stood up as he saw Ella smile at him blushing and picked up his bowl as he sang, "She glanced this way.... I thought I saw." As he walked towards her, he wondered, "And when we touched she didn't shudder at my paw. No, it can't be. I'll just ignore." He shook his head as he neared her, "But, then she's never looked at me that way before." He placed his bowl in front of the chair next to Ella and sat down. As he steadied himself, he saw Ella look away as she smiled. The Beast was about to dip his head down to drink the soup from the bowl but, he hesitated as she was staring at him. He looked up as he looked anywhere but her.

His eyes widened as he saw her remove her spoon from the bowl and place it on the table. She picked up her bowl with both her hands and she nervously glanced at him as she brought the bowl near her mouth and she drank directly from the bowl. She gulped down the soup as she waited for him to drink and the Beast immediately picked up the bowl in his hands as he took a big gulp from the bowl, avoiding her eyes. She followed suit as they both drank from the bowl and as they gulped it down, they placed the bowls on the table together.

Ella chuckled at him as she wiped the corners of her mouth and the Beast smiled nervously at her.

~~~

Ella looked out the library window and she chuckled as she saw the Beast walking the horse around while talking to him animatedly. She sang as she looked at them, "New and a bit alarming. Who'd have ever thought that this could be?" She smiled at him.

She walked away from the window as she placed the ladder at the book shelf and as she climbed it she wondered, "True that he's no Prince Charming." She sang as she took out a few books from the shelf and looked at the window as she continued, "But, there's something in him that I simply didn't see." She stood on the ladder as she smiled to herself and thought about him.

Ella was startled out of her moment as the Beast ventured into the library wearing his waist coat, he smiled as he saw her and made his way over to her as he saw her holding the books in hands. He quickly took the books from her hand and placed them on the pile of books on the table.

Lumière, Mrs. Potts, Mr. Cogsworth, Plumetter and Chip joined them in the library as they saw them working together. They looked at them and wondered out loud. "Well, who'd have known?" Mr. Cogsworth exclaimed as he looked at them. Lumière nodded his head as he agreed, "Well, who indeed?" he tugged Plumette closer as he continued, "And who'd have guessed they'd come together on their own?"

Ella handed the Beast a few more books and shifted the ladder to another book shelf as Mrs. Potts walked towards them as she spoke, "It's so peculiar, wait and see." The others nodded their heads as they agreed, "We'll wait and see a few days more." Ella took out a few more books as she got down from the ladder and walked towards the Beast as she handed him the remaining books and he piled it on the top. She stood next to him and opened a book as they both looked at the synopsis, standing close to each other.

"There may be something there that wasn't there before." They all sang in unison as they made their way out of the library, knowing it was no use as Ella and the Beast were engrossed in their book readings.

Chip turned to Mrs. Potts as he asked in confusion, "What, Mama?"

Mrs. Potts chuckled at his curiosity as she tugged him closer and said, ""There may be something there that wasn't there before."

The servants closed the door behind them as they left Ella and the Beast in their own world of love and reading.

~~~

Beast

The Beast sat at the gardens as he read a book. He wasn't aware as he was busy reading that Ella had walked over to him and looked up as she sat beside him and asked, "What are you reading?" He was startled by her voice as he quickly closed the book and looked everywhere else but her. He muttered quietly as he shook his head, "Nothing."

Ella looked at the book cover and sang out loud, "Guinevere and Lancelot." The Beast stuttered as he turned to look at her and shook his head as he told her, "King Arthur and the Round Table," Ella tried to look interested in his reasons as he continued, "Knights, men, swords and so on." He mumbled as she looked ahead. She smiled cheekily at him as she uttered, "But, still it's a romance." The Beast huffed out as he gave up and agreed, "Alright."

He chuckled as he looked at her but, stopped as she slowly mumbled, "I never thanked you for saving my life." He shook his head as he looked at her said, "Well, I never thanked you for not leaving out for the wolves to eat." She chuckled as she looked at him. The snow surrounding them was beauty and they both seemed odd seating in the garden.

They both looked at the castle as they heard laughter coming from the inside and Ella smiled at the sound as she spoke, "They know how to have a good time." The Beast chuckled as he looked down and shook his head as he spoke, "Well, the laughter dies as soon as I enter the room."

Ella smiled at his foolishness as she said, "Well, my stepmother says that I have ugly skin and am a funny girl." She shook her head as she remembered the memory of her stepmother. The Beast looked at her as her skin glowed in the bright sunlight and appeared golden. He was enchanted by her beauty and he said to her, "You have beautiful skin." Ella stopped smiling as she turned to look at him and found him staring at her with adoring eyes. "Your stepmother is weird and a funny woman as she can't see the beauty when it lies in front of her very own eyes."

The silence that followed suit after his statement left both of them astonished as they quickly looked down after realising what they had been doing. The Beast cleared his throat and he could feel the tension between them so, he tried suggesting an idea, "What do you say we run away?" Ella looked at him confused as he nodded his head towards the library.

They stood up from the bench and walked over to the library. As, the Beast opened the doors of the library, Ella gasped as she still wasn't used to seeing the library every day. She waited at the table for the Beast as he climbed up the ladder and pulled out a big book from the shelf and held it in his hand. He climbed down the ladder and walked over to where she stood and set it on the book stand. He opened the book to its centre page and stood back as he let Ella take a look at the book.

She gasped at the magical book and felt her pages in her hand. She turned towards him as she said, "It's gorgeous." He shrugged at her as he spoke, "Another gift by the Enchantress. It was the cruellest trick of all." Ella looked at him confused as she couldn't decipher what he was trying to say.

The Beast nodded at her as he took a step forward and stood next to her, "You see, this book can take you anytime, anywhere." Ella gasped at the book and he continued, "But, no one wanted me. Anywhere I went, they all despised me because of the way I looked and treated me worse than an animal." His voice became low at the end as he stared down at his fur coated hands. The claws reminding him of the monster he was. Ella looked at him but, sympathy wasn't what Beast saw in her eyes when he looked up at her as she touched his arm; it was love and affection. "The world has no place for a monster like me." He said as he took her hands in his, "But, it can for you."

Although, she never talked about it but, he could see it in her eyes. He cleared his throat as he spoke, "Think of the one place you've always wanted to see." He told her as he placed their joined hands on the page of the book and saw her deep in her thoughts.

He withdrew his hand as he said, "Now, find it in your mind's eye." He nodded at her as she looked up at him, "And then feel it in your heart." They both closed their eyes as Ella thought of the place she always wanted to see.

They both opened their eyes to find themselves in an apartment. The room was cold and dark as the lamps were blown out and the cold wind that flowed through the windows, made them shiver. The Beast walked towards the window and he held the curtains in his hands as he looked out. He saw the city of Paris in front of his and he smiled as he asked us, "You took us to Paris? Why, Paris though? Do you want to start by visiting the tourists place? There are a lot of beautiful places around here." The Beast stopped talking as he glanced back at Ella to find her looking around the room.

Ella bent down as she picked up something and she cried as she held it in her hands. She turned to look at him as she spoke, "This is where my Papa died." They heard voices coming from the room next to them and they both stared at each other before they quietly made their way over there. As they neared the door, Ella walked in the front and the Beast followed her footsteps.

Ella touched the wall as she bent down slightly to look into the dimly lit room. She gasped as she saw her father in the bed coughing up blood as he rested in the bed. Ella couldn't believe her eyes as she saw a doctor seating next to her father's bed. "It's Papa." She whispered lightly and the Beast's eyes widened as they stared at the sight in front of them. They saw as the doctor injected some medicine into her father's hand and her father tried denying it but to no avail. The medicine had already been injected and her father was slowly leaving his conscious state of mind. They saw as the tables were covered in medicine bottles and tablets were spread all around the room with tissue covering the floor.

Ella took a step back as she saw her father look at her but, she quickly looked back in as she heard another voice speak up, "Tell me where your daughter is?" Ella's eyes widened as she saw her stepmother walk around her Papa's bed and her Papa's eyes followed her movements. "It's my stepmother." Ella whispered to the Beast and the reality seemed strange for him.

Ella's father shook his head as he struggled speak, "I don't know where she is." Her stepmother stopped in her tracks as she turned towards her father and screamed, "Don't lie to me." Her father cried as the doctor inserted another injection into his arm and spoke, "I really don't know." The stepmother looked at him in disgust as she spat at him, "Then where has she ran off to?" Her father cried and Ella's breathing stopped as she saw him in such pain. The evil stepmother shook her head at him and looked at the doctor as she spoke, "Just do it already."

Ella's eyes widened as she saw the doctor take out another injection and put it in her father's hand. Her father screamed in pain as the needle injected him and he looked at Ella with fearful eyes as he closed his eyes suddenly and his limbs lost their strength.

Ella cried out loud as she saw her father die in front of her and the Beast quickly muffled her screams with his hands as he couldn't risk them being found by the evil stepmother and stepped back. He struggled to hold Ella in his arms as she broke down crying and she stepped towards her father's room. He cradled her as she broke down and the Beast's eyes widened as he heard footsteps approaching them. He quickly hugged her as he muttered, "I'm sorry." Before he closed his eyes and made their way back to the castle.

~~~

"la nuit magique"

Third POV

The Beast sighed out loud as he scratched his back with the help of the brush. Lumière sighed from the other side of the curtain which separated them and Lumière was forever greatly for that as he didn't want to see his Master naked. Mrs. Potts stood next to him as they both saw their Master getting more nervous as the seconds passed. "Why did I ask her?" His Master groaned from the bath tub as he rubbed soap onto his fur.

Lumière chuckled lightly at Plumette who looked away from her the bath tub. "I mean I just asked her casually, would you like to join me for a dance? Why did she had to agree to it?" His Master asked as he stood up from the bath groaning out loud and shook his head. Plumette screamed as her eyes bulged out as she took her Master in. Lumière quickly closed her eyes with his hands as he shrieked at his Master, "Master, cover yourself."

The Beast's eyes widened as he realised that he had stood up naked in front of his servants and quickly covered himself with the cloth that the coat hanger handed him. He looked around nervously as he chuckled lightly, "Sorry." He wore his bath robe as he walked over to his closet and took out a dark blue suit from the closet and placed it on the bed. He returned to the dressing table where he saw that Plumette had recovered from the shocks of seeing him naked and he apologised once again.

He sat down in the chair in front of his dressing table. All his servants surrounded him as he looked at himself in the mirror. "What was I thinking?" He wondered out loud once again and Lumière replied, "No, master. It's perfect. The rose has only four petals left which means you can tell her how you feel." Beast shook his head at Lumière as he spoke, "I feel like a fool." Lumière smiled at him slightly as he said, "Do not be discouraged, Master." The Beast looked at Lumière as if he had grown three heads, "She will never love me." Lumière shook his head, "She is the one."

The Beast groaned as he spoke, "Please, stop saying that. There is no 'one.'" He huffed out at Lumière. Lumière jumped onto his chair as he leaned down he asked, "You care for her, don't you?" The Beast nodded as his reply and looked at his reflection. "Well, then woo her with beautiful music and romantic candlelit dinner."

Plumette flew in front of him as she giggled, "And when the moments just right, tell her." The Beast sighed as he looked at them, "How will I know?" Mr. Cogsworth looked at him as he coughed, "You'll feel slightly nauseous." Lumière patted his shoulder as he spoke, "Don't worry, Master. You'll do fine." The Beast rolled his eyes at Lumière as he knew he wouldn't do fine.

The Beast turned to look at Mrs. Potts as she spoke, "Just don't be so nervous and tell Ella how you feel." She looked at him sweetly but then her face grew angrier as she spat at him, "Because if you don't, I promise you'll be drinking cold tea for the rest of your days!" The Beast's eyes widened as he looked at Lumière, "In the dark." Plumette stood next to him as she finished for them, "Covered in dust."

"Dark and very, very dirty." Lumière said as he clapped his arms together and Beast seemed frightened and confused.

Lumière looked at the coat hanger as he started, "Start with the hair." Mr. Cogsworth handed the coat hanger the hair brush and the coat hanger looked at the Beast as she clicked his scissors together, "Woman love nice hair!" The coat hanger turned the Beast's chair around as Mrs. Potts said, "Now, tidy the fingers and toes." She poured the Master a cup of hot tea and he placed his fingers one by one into the hot cup of tea. Mr. Cogsworth looked at the Beast as he turned towards the coat hanger and said, "Chapeau, brush those teeth. They need it."

Chapeau cut off his Master's beard as Mrs. Potts steamed the nails. Lumière spoke, "Polish the nails." As he cleaned the horns on his Master's head with the help of a cloth, "Shine the horns." Plumette picked up the powder puff as she spoke, "Eyes closed." The Beast closed his eyes and heard her say, "Puff, puff." As she powdered his face. The Beast coughed out some of the powder from his mouth and sneezed out loud. Lumière turned his chair around as Mrs. Potts looked at the Beast and her and Chips's eyes widened as they realised how weird the Beast looked. The Beast smiled at them with his fangs on display and Lumière sighed as he folded his hands in front of him, "Okay. I can fix this." The Beast gave up as he looked down and sighed loudly.

~~~

Ella smiled lightly as she turned around in her place. She saw as Madame Garderobe gasped at her as she exclaimed, "Oh beautiful!" As she took a look over Ella, she said, "But, there's something missing." She waved her hands in the air and the gold decorations along the ceiling flew in the air and settled on Ella's yellow bright dress. They covered the bottom part of her dress and Ella smiled as she remembered her fairy godmother who had helped her get ready for the Royal Ball. She nodded at Madam Garderobe as she walked to the side of her bed and opened the drawer to reveal the shoes she had managed to save as the magic has changed everything back to normal. She put them on as she smiled at Madame Garderobe who gushed at how beautiful Ella looked.

Ella smiled remembering her mother and how she always said that Yellow colour suited her perfect golden brown skin tone. She thanked Madame Garderobe as she made her way out of her bedroom and towards the Ball room.

~~~

Ella and the Beast both stared at each other as they stood on the opposite sides of the balcony. The position reminded them both of the night of the Royal Ball when Ella had walked into the room full of people and still managed to catch the Beast's eyes. She was the most beautiful woman in the world, he thought.

They both smiled at each other nervously as they started walking down the stairs at the same time. They reached at the ending of the stair case and the Beast held his arm in the air, waiting for Ella to link her hand through it. Ella looked at his arm and smiled as she linked her left arm through his right. The Beast sighed in relief as Ella didn't reject his offer. They slowly took the remaining steps one at a time as they reached the floor.

Lumière, Mrs. Potts and Mr. Cogsworth, Plumette and Chip stood on the Maestro Cadanza's head board as they stared at the two awkward, nervous birdies making their way into the Ball room. The Ball room was dusted off and lit with the lamps and the lanterns as Plumette had made sure of it. Mrs. Potts started singing as Maestro Cadanza played the music on his piano. "Tale as old as time." Mrs. Potts saw as both of them walked towards the centre of the Ball room, "True as it can be. Barely even friends, then somebody bends unexpectedly." They stood in front of each other as they reached the centre of the ballroom.

They both glanced around the lit Ball room as they nervously glanced at each other. Ella held her gown as she bowed down in front of the Beast and he was startled at her brave nature, even though he should be used to it by now, he thought. He bowed down in front of her as she stood up and as he stood up straight she saw Ella holding her hands in the air, waiting for him to guide her through it.

"Just a little change, small to say the least. Neither one prepared, Beauty and the Beast." Mrs. Potts sang as she saw Beast take Ella's hand in his and he walked her through the music as he tugged her closer to him.

"Ever just the same." The Beast twirled Ella around in his arms as she smiled gracefully at him, "Ever a surprise." He smiled at her as he held her hand and placed his other hand behind his back as they danced together. "Ever as sure."

"As the sun will rise." The Beast circled Ella around his arms as he didn't turn his gaze anywhere else even for a moment.

"Tale as old as time. Song as old as rhyme." The beast let go of Ella's hand as he let her circle around herself as her gown danced along with her. "Bittersweet and strange. Finding you can change." Mrs. Potts continued singing as she saw the two dance together.

"Learning you were wrong." The Beast tugged Ella closer as he took her right hand in his left and she placed her left hand on his shoulders, he curved his right hand along her waist and pulled her closer as she gasped a little.

He pulled her closer as he let go of her hands and she circled them around his neck; the Beast dipped Ella down as he held her in his arms. Their faces were mere inches away and one move from one of them and they would kiss. But, the Beast suddenly lifted Ella in his right hand and twirled her around in the air as they never broke their gaze. The Ball room's lights dimmed as he placed her back on the floor and took her hands in his again. "Certain as the sun."

"Rising in the east." They both circled around each other as they danced around the Ball room. "Tale as old as time. Song as old as rhyme." They slowed down their dancing as the music slowly came to a halt. They both stood next to each other as the Beast held his arm up once again and Ella quickly linked her arm through his as they heard Mrs. Potts finish the song.

"Beauty and the Beast."

Maestro Cadanza finished the song with a key note as they both made their way to the balcony, arms linked with one another. They both smiled to one another as they reached the balcony and walked onto the snow. The Beast glanced back at the Ball room and knew that he's servants were waiting for him to confess. So, he cleared his throat as he looked at her. She turned her head towards him as she waited for him to speak, "I...I have wanting to ask something of you." The beast started as he looked at her nervously, "Is there any chance that a creature like me to hope that he may be able to earn your affection?" He stared at her as he waited for her answer. He gulped nervously as she shrugged at him, "I don't know." He couldn't believe his eyes as he stared at her with wide eyes. He leaned towards her as he asked her, "Do you think you could be happy here?"

Ella stared straight as she thought and asked, "Can anyone be happy if they aren't free?" The Beast took a step back as he realised he had taken her prisoner all this time and she couldn't leave the castle. He looked ahead as he stared at the dark veil of the night and couldn't answer her question. The silence between them seemed uncertain.

Ella broke the silence as she spoke, "My father taught me how to dance in our house." The beast turned towards her as she continued, "I used to step on his toes a lot." She smiled at his sweet memory, "The only thing I have of him is my home." The Beast looked at her as he said, "You must miss it a lot."

Ella nodded her head at his statement as she blinked back tears, "I do." Beast couldn't see her sad as he asked, "Do you want to see your house?" She turned towards him in confusion and he nodded at her to follow him. They both rushed towards his bedroom as the night grew darker.

They reached his bedroom and made their way to the rose on the balcony. The Beast picked up the magical mirror from the table and gave it to her as he nodded.

Ella took the mirror reluctantly as she stared at the mirror and spoke, "I'd like to see my house." The mirror waved as the water and the reflection changed to her house. Ella gasped as she saw Lady Tremaine and her daughters standing outside her house and a crowd shouting at a person. She scrunched her face in confusion as she stared at the person, but as they turned around she realised it was her father. She gasped out loud as she gestured at the Beast, "Papa! My father! He's alive."

She showed him the mirror and the Beast's brows furrowed as he remembered him dying in Paris. Ella continued as she looked at the mirror, "And he's in trouble. He's hurt." The beast turned away from her as he looked down and said, "Then you must go." Ella looked up to the Beast as the reflection in the mirror returned as Ella stared at the Beast in disbelief, "What did you say?"

The Beast turned to look at her as he mustered his courage and said, "You must go to him. No time to waste." Ella breathed heavily as she handed the Beast the mirror back, her face full of confusion. "No." The beast denied as she refused to take the mirror back, "Keep with you. And you'll always have a way to look back at me." He smiled lightly at her as he placed the mirror in her hands and nodded. Ella took a step back hesitantly as she stared at him. She looked down as she stared at her glass slippers and she took them off, the Beast stared at her in confusion as she picked them up in her hands. She sighed as she looked at them and she thrusted them towards him as she spoke, "These are very special to me. These were given to me by the fairy godmother. Please, take care of them." She smiled sadly at him as she gave the slippers to him and took a step back. The Beast's gaze was fixated on them as they sparkled in the dim moonlight. He smiled at her as he nodded and spoke, "I promise to take care of them. I'll keep them safe in my heart." She nodded hesitantly as she walked back slowly.

"Thank you." She said as she turned around and stepped forward. She walked towards the doors fast but, she turned around one last time to glance at him and he smiled lightly at her. She took that as a cue to leave as she gathered her gown in her hands and ran.

The Beast looked as she ran further away from him but, he couldn't do anything else. Ella reached the staircase leading to the main door and she rushed down the stairs. She stopped as she met Chapeau, the coat hanger and she bowed in front of him as a final respect and looked around the castle, before she stepped her foot out of the main door and she climbed on her horse. Mrs. Potts saw Ella leave through the main door and her heart hurt.

Cogsworth, Lumière and Mrs. Potts walked into their Master's bedroom as they saw him standing near the rose. "Well, Master. I have had my doubts, but everything's moving like a clockwork. True love really wins the day!" Cogsworth exclaimed as he swung his arm in the air.

The Beast didn't meet their gaze as he looked down and hesitantly replied, "I let her go." They all gasped at his statement as Lumière asked him, "What? How could do that, Master?" The Beast looked at them as he replied, "I had to. I'm sorry I couldn't set you free as I did to her." He apologised to them as he paced around the rose, the glass slippers sitting next to it on the table. The servants gazed at it questioning as they saw him touch it slowly.

"But, why?" Cogsworth questioned him and he kept quite as he looked out in the night and saw Ella ride the horse as she reached the entrance of the castle.

"Because he loves her." Mrs. Potts replied for him and they took his silence as a cue to leave.

~~~

Lady Tremaine

Lady Tremaine smirked at her husband who was soon going to be her ex-husband and give her all his property which he had named in Ella's name. She tugged on the cloth tied tightly around his neck as she smiled sweetly at him as her two daughters stood behind her. She placed her shotgun at his neck as she asked him, "Where is Ella?"

"I don't know." Ella's father shrieked loudly as much as he could with the cloth tied around his mouth. He looked at her as she shook her head, "Wrong choice." Her girls laughed out loud behind evilly as she held the gun higher to his head and shot the gun. Her father closed his eyes anticipating the bullet to hit him but, nothing happened as the gun was empty and only the sound of the gun was heard as they laughed evilly at his expense.

They stopped laughing as they heard a knock on the door. Lady Tremaine straightened up as she said, "This is not your fate, darling." She gestured at the gun and then pointed at the door as Drizella walked over to open the door, "But, that is." Just as Drizella opened the door, Lady Tremaine placed the gun in Ella's father's lap and started crying loudly as she saw people enter the house. She cried as she made weird hand gestures around her, "He... he" She said through her tears as she sobbed, "He tried killing me with the gun."

The Villagers gasped at her sobs and they turned towards him as they angrily approached him. He shook his head violently at them as she said, "See, he even has the audacity to deny it." She sobbed as the Villagers pulled him up from the chair and walked him out of the house. He saw his ex-servants standing in the crowd with their heads hung in shame.

The cloth around Ella's father's mouth loosened and he shouted, "I didn't try to kill her. She tried to kill me." He pointed his shivering finger at Lady Tremaine and she sobbed more trying to convince the crowd of her innocent self.

"He's gone mad after Ella ran off somewhere." Lady Tremaine sobbed as she looked at the Villagers and they nodded their heads at her as they held him in his place, as Ella's father struggled against their holds.

He shook his head violently at them to convince them of her wrong doings but, the Villagers believed the lady who was a sobbing mess and not a father who had supposedly gone mad after his daughter went missing.

"He needs treatment." Lady Tremaine said as she looked around the Villagers and they agreed to her, she smirked lightly at Ella's father and then her smirk changed to a smile of gratitude as she thanked the Villagers for their support.

Lady Tremaine turned towards the doctor and smiled at him graciously as she asked him, "Would you please help us doctor?" Lady Tremaine walked towards her husband and stood behind him as they sat him in the wheelchair. She placed her hands on his shoulders and massaged his shoulders as she leaned down to whisper in his ears, "This is your last chance, darling. Wouldn't want to spend the last of your days in the mental asylum, would you?" His eyes widened as he stared at the carriage they brought in to transport him to the mental asylum.

For the Villagers, it looked like Lady Tremaine was whispering sweet nothings to calm him down, but she was threatening to kill him if he didn't tell her where Ella was.

Lady Tremaine walked around her husband as she smiled at him innocently and then bent down in front of him. She placed her palm on his knees as she caressed his thighs and asked him, "Where is Ella?" He shook his head as he muttered crying, "I...I...don't know. I really don't know." He cried out in vain as her finger nails dug deep into his skin as she clenched his thigh, causing the blood to spill out. "Please, let me go. Please, let me go. You can have all the money and property you want but, please let me." Her father pleaded as he looked at her but, she shook her head as she stood up from the ground and turned around abruptly.

Ella's father knew his wife's strange addiction with Ella had something to do with the glass slippers, they were worth a ton of gold and she wanted to keep them to herself. He still wasn't sure as to why she thought he knew his daughter's whereabouts since he had seen her last on the day of his trip. He had no idea of the said Royal Ball, neither did he know that his daughter had went there in a disguise, this was what Lady Tremaine had been telling him since the last few days. As, Ella apparently went missing after the night of the Royal Ball.

He struggled as the doctor's men/nurses forced him to stand up and pushed him towards the enclosed carriage. The carriage from outside looked like it was used to lock prisoners or thieves. The doctor smirked at him as he bowed in front of him and held his hand as the nurses forced him to step his foot forward. Ella's father lost his balance as he fell forward and the doctor gripped his shoulders, stabling him. The doctor turned towards the Villagers as he said, "I'm going to help this poor soul be human again."

The Villagers awed at his great courage and Ella's father shook their head at them as his body shook from the medicine, the doctor had injected into his shoulder, his hand hid from the Villagers.

He pushed Ella's father into the carriage and shut the door as he heard a horse neighing loudly as the doctor stepped back from the carriage. As he bent his head forward he saw the "missing" Ella riding her way to the carriage on a horse in a bright yellow gown.

Lady Tremaine's eyes widened as she took stepped towards her step daughter in delight. Lady Tremaine's heart felt joy as she saw her future fortune get down from the horse hurriedly. She was huffing and out of breath as she rushed towards the carriage. Ella stepped on the ladder as she looked at her father through the bar sills in the door and exclaimed, "Papa!" Her father who was sitting down defeated stood up straight as he heard his daughter's voice. He touched the bar sills and he looked at his daughter with tearful eyes. He wasn't sure if would be able to see her again. He was scared he had lost her too.

"Ella, my love." He sobbed as he touched her cheeks with the sills separating them. Ella's eyes were damped too as she looked at her father and the image of him dying from the night in Paris flashed in front of her eyes. She thought she was dreaming as the image of him laying lifeless on the bed in the dark night didn't seem to leave her mind. But, as soon as her father's fingers touched her cheeks, the warmth in her heart returned as she cried happy tears and chuckled at him through her tears, "It really is you." She smiled at her and she felt her heart clustering as he smiled back at her through his sobs and nodded as his reply.

She nodded at him as she wiped her tears with the back of her hands and stepped away from the carriage and turned around to face her stepmother and the Villagers. They all stared at her as if she was a ghost and were too stunned to speak. Ella looked at her stepmother's tear stained face and saw her smile at her. Ella stepped towards her as she remembered her from the night of Paris and the sight of her telling the doctor to inject her father floated in her mind. Ella gasped as she felt her stepmother run towards her and hug her tightly. Ella didn't return the hug back as her hands were shivering from witnessing the selfishness and greediness of the woman she knew as her stepmother.

She stared in disbelief as her stepmother released her from her hold and stepped back as she looked at her adoringly and wiped fake tears as she said to the Villagers, "My daughter is finally home." Ella cringed at the word daughter as she knew the word meant nothing to her stepmother. The woman could never be a proper mother. She knew nothing about the greatness of being a mother. What great responsibilities came with being a mother? No, all she knew was luxury and gold.

Ella didn't show any emotions as she was angry and hurt a million times by this woman but, she kept her emotions at a bay as she rehearsed her mother's teachings – Have courage and be kind.

As Lady Tremaine finished her fake drama she turned towards Ella, "Where were you my child?" Ella felt bile rising in her throat as she heard the sweet calling and she teared her hand away from her chin as she asked her, "Why is Papa in that carriage? What did you do to him?" She asked as she narrowed her eyes and Lady Tremaine looked taken back as she heard Ella talk back to her in front of the crowd.

She gasped as she placed her hand on her chest, "You think I would put my own husband in a mental hospital? Why would I do that to my own husband?" Lady Tremaine held Ella's hand as she noticed the mirror in her hand. She eyed it suspiciously as she asked Ella, "Where were you all these days? We were worried sick."

Ella eyed the crowd as she looked around and saw her father looking at her sadly through the sill, before she gathered her strength to speak, "I was at the castle."

"Which castle, love?" Lady Tremaine asked as she stepped closer to Ella, "The castle vanished in the air when we left the Royal Ball. How were you living there?" She asked as she knew Ella was in a vulnerable position due to her father's state.

Ella looked at her father as she spoke, "I was taken as a prisoner by the Beast." The crowd gasped in horror at her revealing and Lady Tremaine's interest peaked as she nodded her to continue, "He let me go as I saw that my father was in trouble."

Lady Tremaine arched her brow as she said, "There is no Beast." She laughed loudly as she continued, "Those are just fairy tales for children, Ella. Grow up." The crowd laughed with her as they stared at the wide eyed girl in the centre. "And even though this said Beast is alive, how did you see that your father was in trouble?" Lady Tremaine asked as smiled lightly at Ella's confused self.

Ella clenched the mirror tighter in her hand as she brought it up and gulped nervously as she saw every gaze was fixated on her. She looked at her reflection in the mirror as she muttered the words, "Show me the Beast." The reflection in the mirror blurred as it changed and showed her the insights of the Beast standing near the rose as he held the glass slipper in his hand and looked at it sadly.

Ella smiled sadly at his image as she flipped the mirror around for her stepmother to see and the Villagers gasped as they saw the hideous looking beast with his huge fangs and black horns, the fur covering every inch of his skin.

Lady Tremaine's interest peeked as she took the mirror in her hands and her smile widened as she saw the glass slipper in his hand. She looked up at Ella who was now standing near the bar sills on the carriage, talking to her father. "It was you, wasn't it?" She asked Ella and she turned to her confused as she asked, "What?" "The girl at the Royal Ball. The mysterious girl with the glass slippers." Lady Tremaine smirked at her as she revealed her secret.

Ella's eyes widened in surprise as she looked around the crowd and saw them mumbling to one another about the Royal Ball. Lady Tremaine now clenched the mirror tightly in her hand as she spoke, "I knew it was no mere coincidence that you disappeared on the same night of the Royal Ball." She walked towards her and Ella was confused as she looked at her, "You and the Beast were planning our ruination at the castle." Lady Tremaine exclaimed accusingly as she pointed the mirror at Ella and Ella's eyes widened as she shook her head at her denying the accusation.

Lady Tremaine flipped the mirror for the Villagers to see the horrid image of the Beast and exclaimed as they gasped in horror at the Beast, "Look at him. Look at him as he would kidnap all your children and then eat them one by one as he will please himself." She walked around the crowd as she continued, "And when he will be bored with the children he will come for the adults. He will tear the flesh off your bones as he will devour every single person in the village and no one will be alive."

The crowd were horrified as they heard Lady Tremaine spoke of the things the Beast would do to them and they stepped away from the mirror as they feared he would jump out of the mirror. Ella shook her head as she shouted, "No! No! The Beast, he is nice, he is kind and caring. He won't do any of these things she just said." Ella struggled as she was held by the doctor as she tried snatching the mirror from her stepmother's hands.

Lady Tremaine turned towards her in an angry stance as she pointed at her and shrieked, "Look at her! He has charmed her with his magic and now she's asking us to leave him alone." Lady Tremaine looked around with blazing fire as she exclaimed, "We have to kill the Beast!"

The Villagers nodded their head in agreement as they murmured their answers and Ella cried in vain as she saw Lady Tremaine holding her shot gun in her hands, "He is innocent! Leave him alone." She tried releasing her hands from their hold but, she was not strong enough as they tightened their grip on her every time she moved, "Please don't kill him."

Lady Tremaine stood in front of Ella as she bent her head to speak, "I'm sorry, little Ella. But, we have to kill your love as I want those glass slippers." She stood up straight as she told the doctor, "Lock her up with her father."

The doctor nodded at her as he smirked and opened the carriage door and threw her inside as he locked the door from outside. Ella scrambled to her feet as soon as she hit the ground and looked through the bar sills as Lady Tremaine exclaimed out loud encouraging the Villagers to sharpen their tools, "We have to kill the Beast!"

Lady Tremaine held the shot gun in her left hand and the magical mirror in her right, as the Villagers stood behind her as she said, "Show me the way to the castle." She smirked as her reflection in the mirror faded and the path leading to the castle appeared in front of her eyes.

"Let's kill the Beast!" She exclaimed and started her journey to the castle.

~~~

Moment de vérité - I

Lumière's POV

Lumière glanced at Mrs. Potts as he held Plumette's hand. He turned back to her as she sighed. He knew she was upset as they had no choice but to await their faith. He looked at her adoringly as she smiled up to him sadly. He had to see her till their so called death by the rose. They were anticipating the fall of the last petal. But, that didn't mean they couldn't enjoy their last moments. So, Lumière tugged Plumette closer as he placed his right hand on her waist. Plumette smiled at the closeness and sighed as she placed her head on his chest as he twirled them around.

"At least, he finally learned to love." Lumière announced as they danced around the fireplace and everyone around them nodded their head at him.

Mr. Cogsworth however huffed as he stood in an angry stance, "But, what good is it? Since, she clearly doesn't love him back." He walked towards the window as his shoulders slung down in disappointment.

Mrs. Potts looked at them as she said, "She loves him. There's still time as there are two petals left on the rose. What if she came back?" She asked around and she saw a little hope on their faces, "Be patient." She nodded as she smiled sadly.

Chips stood next to her as he heard something from the woods. He exclaimed as he jumped in his place, "Did you hear that, Mama?" He looked at her expectedly as he asked, "Is she coming back?" He jumped towards the fog covered window to look outside.

Lumière's ears perked up at this as he quickly climbed the window and wiped the fog on the window as he strained his eyes to look more clearly. Mrs. Potts stood next to her son as she too peered out of the window, hoping for the return of the beloved Ella. She had grown close to her these past few days and she loved the fact that she brought Master's good side.

Mr. Cogsworth struggled as he slowly climbed the window with the help of Lumière because of his old age. He walked slowly towards the sill as he huffed out breath, trying to calm his breathing. "Well, at last she thought of us." He grumbled out. Plumette flew next to him as she looked through window as she was high in the air.

Suddenly, Lumière saw the fire torches in the woods and he squinted his eyes as the view cleared in front of him and he exclaimed, "Invaders! They are coming for us!" Everyone was on high alert as they themselves saw the mob. The mob was angry as they held the torches high in the air and roared out as they headed towards the castle.

"Barricade the entrance!" Mr. Cogsworth exclaimed as they all got down from the window and headed towards the entrance. Mr. Cogsworth ran as fast as he could and Lumière was the first to reach the doors. They could hear the shouting of the mob from outside. Mrs. Potts and Chapeau rushed to the door.

They could sense the Mob getting closer to them as the seconds passed. The main door was locked and there was no way they get in. Maestro

Cadanza came running as he climbed down the staircase and yelled, "I'll barricade them." He quickly stood on two of his supports and hugged the main door as the Mob from outside started pounding on the door. He hugged the door tightly as the door started moving a little due to the pounding. All were anxious as they heard how angry the Mob was and they weren't sure if they would be able to stop them but, nonetheless they held their stance.

The pounding on the door suddenly stopped and Lumière let out a breath of relief as he thought that the Mob had left. But, a moment later Mr. Cogsworth gasped out loud in shock as the Mob suddenly pounded the small door on the main door and the wood door broke in pieces as they hit it again. Maestro Cadanza lost his balance due to the impact as he fell backwards but, Chapeau was quick to catch him. Mrs. Potts gasped out loud at the intruders and Chip was scared as he looked at Lumière.

Lumière looked towards the west wing as he quickly thought of a plan. He looked at Mr. Cogsworth as he ushered him and whispered in his ear. Mr. Cogsworth quickly nodded at him as he rushed as fast as he could towards the west wing. Lumière looked back at the door and nodded at others as he said, "We got work to do."

~~~

Mr. Cogsworth's POV

Mr. Cogsworth huffed out a breath as he tried to climb the staircase as fast as he could to his Master's bedroom. He smiled nervously as he reached the doors to his Master's bedroom. He opened the doors to meet with nothing. His master was no were to be seen, so he walked further into the room. He searched every corner of the room and then he heard weeping. He walked towards the sound and his eyes widened as he took in his Master's scrunched down figure in the balcony holding the glass slipper as he wept.

His heart broke as he walked towards his Master. He cautiously stepped closer to him as he didn't want to anger him. He cleared his throat and his Master, turned sideways as he looked at him. "Master, they are breaking down the door. We have to do something." His Master shrugged at him as he shook his head, "Let them break it. We don't have enough time anyway." His Master stood up as he clenched the glass slipper in his hand and looked at the dark night. The cold breeze hit his face like a sharp strike and he shivered from it, as he realised it was the beginning of the end.

Mr. Cogsworth stared at his Master in disbelief as he knew his Master wasn't one to give up so easily. He realised that it was their turn to save him from the unknown monster. He nodded at him and took his leave, even though he knew his Master was paying no mind to him.

~~~

Third POV

Lumière stood as still as he could as the castle was silent, and the only noise could be heard was of the intruders who had stepped in the castle. He opened his left eye as he spied on them. The intruders were the Villagers and they were confused as they looked around the castle.

He heard one of the girls, he tried to recall her name, maybe it was Drizella or Anastasia, he thought. She shivered as she looked frightened, "Mother, did it ever occur to you that maybe this castle would be haunted?" The other sister hit her with the torch on her head and snickered, "You believe in these stories, Drizella? See, this is why you're so dumb." She cringed at her sister's nonsense talks and walked towards the table where Mrs. Potts and Chips sat on.

Their mother Lady Tremaine walked cautiously around the foyer as she ignored her idiotic daughters and looked around to find any traces of the Beast. She rolled her eyes as she heard the scarred whispers of the Villagers.

She heard Mr. Pott wonder out loud as he touched the pillar, "This place seems familiar. It's like I have been here before." A few others nodded at his thought as they roamed in the foyer. The castle was silent other than their whisperings and Chapeau opened his right eye to see their movements

As Anastasia walked towards Mrs. Potts she bent down as she touched Chip and patted his head as she muttered, "Oh, you must be the talking tea-cup, Chip." Drizella rolled her eyes at her sister as she had warned her not to believe in fairy tales, but here she was talking to the imaginary talking tea-cup. Anastasia turned towards Mrs. Potts and spoke, "And you must be his grandmother."

Mrs. Potts gasped out loud as she shrieked loudly and opened her eyes, "Grandmother?" She exclaimed as he announced, "Attack!" At her command, every object in the castle came to life and started attacking the intruders.

~~~

Ella's POV

Ella sat anxiously in the carriage as she fidgeted in her place. She stood up suddenly not able to control her impatience, "I have to warn the beast." Her father looked at her concerned as he asked her, "Warn the beast? How did you get away from him?" Ella turned to look at her father as she furrowed her brows, "You knew about the beast, Papa?" She asked him, still not believing her own father.

Her father nodded at her as she sat down in front of him. Ella looked at her father expectantly, as she waited for him to explain. "You see, Ella. The rose I sent you from my journey was from the forest and I knew it had magical powers." Ella looked at him confused as she realised she had been watering the rose ever since and it hadn't wittered at all. But, she wasn't sure of the last few days as she knew her stepsisters would happily peel off the petals; to play with it.

"It was the reason I had been alive for so many days, even though your stepmother had been feeding me less than a normal person needing." He sighed as he looked down and hugged himself as he spoke, "Why didn't I see this coming? I was such a fool." Her father admitted and Ella shook her head as she took his hand in hers and caressed his palm as she spoke, "It wasn't your fault, Papa. She's just a horrible woman." He looked up at her in surprise and she nodded her head.

"I'm so sorry, Ella. She treated you so bad. You didn't deserve it." He apologised to her as he squeezed her hands. A tear fell down his cheeks and Ella immediately wiped it with the back of her hand as she smiled at him, "It's okay, Papa. It's not your fault. What matters most right now that we are together."

"But, we need to stop her right now, Papa. Or else she'll kill him." Ella reasoned out as she pleaded her father to help her out. "Why do you want to help him, Ella? Didn't he take you as his prisoner?" Her father asked he had heard the rumours of Ella going missing near the castle. The people whispered that she was probably dead by now, but for some reason he couldn't bring himself to believe that. One day, he had heard the whisperings of the Beast living in the castle from the nurses and he had put two and two together and everything was clearer than the crystals.

"I believed that you were no longer alive, Papa. But, I saw you. I saw you in Paris." Ella told him the truth as she smiled at him, he scrunched his brows in confusion as he stared at her and asked, "But how?"

"He took me there." Ella said with hope glistering in her eyes. "I saw everything." Her father looked at her sadly as he said, "So, you know why I couldn't come back for you?" Ella nodded her head vigorously as she smiled. "Thank, heavens." Her father said as he kissed her forehead.

"We have to help him, Papa." Ella said as she hugged him. "It's dangerous, my love." Her father reasoned out as he feared for his daughter's life. "I know, it's dangerous, but I'm willing to take the risk." Ella said as she wiped her tears and looked at him hopefully.

Her father stood up as he said, "I mean, I can try to pick the lock? After all, it's just gears and springs." He glided his hands through the bar sills and touched around for the lock. He grinned as he found the lock and touched around to understand its built.

Ella quickly took out a hair pin from her hair and she waited for her father to turn around. As he turned around and said, "I need something long and sharp." She handed him the hair pin and smiled at him. "Just like this." He said as he took the pin and nodded at her.

He continued working on the lock and after a moment, the lock clicked open. He quickly but, without making any noise opened the door and they both stepped out of the carriage. They looked around for the doctor but, he wasn't in front of them. They could hear him though, so they quickly shut the door behind them and Ella ran towards her horse.

She quickly tore off the excess skirt of her gown and climbed the horse. Her father waited for the doctor. He was making a distraction for her. The doctor suddenly appeared in front of the carriage as he searched for the lock and met with an empty carriage. As he closed the door, he was met with Ella's father who quite innocently stood there holding the lock in his palm. He asked him, "Are you looking for this?" The doctor looked at him in confusion, as Ella's father handed him the lock. They both turned towards the sound of the horse neighing and saw Ella ride the horse towards the castle hurriedly. Ella smiled at her father as she waved, "Bye, Papa!"

"Good luck, Ella!" Her father exclaimed as he waved at her; the doctor stood there dumbfounded. "She's very headstrong." He reasoned out nodding his head as the doctor stood there too shocked to say anything.

"Do you have any children?" Ella's father asked as he saw her retreating form.

~~~

Moment de vérité - II

Ella's POV

Ella looked back at her father as she rode the horse. He smiled at her as he waved and she knew she was the luckiest daughter on the planet. Even though, there weren't many moments they had shared but, she knew he adored her as the same as her mother did.

She smiled at him as she turned to look at the road ahead of her. The castle awaiting her presence as she quickened her pace. The Village was silent as no one was present in the Village and the silence deemed on her as she rode towards the forest.

As she entered the forest, she heard the howling of the wolves and shivered as the cold of the night crept on her like a second skin. She tightened the robes around herself as she slapped the ropes fast against the horse's back. The horse obeyed her command as he ran faster in the slippery snow. Ella feared for her life as the howling sounds sounded near but, she ignored them as she looked up at the moon. The moon shone bright and lit the pathway for her. She remembered the last time she was in the same spot and smiled lightly as she recalled the moment, she had decided to help him.

The moonlight shone brightly and so did Ella's smile as she rode towards the castle.

~~~

Lumière's POV

The foyer was a chaos as the servants had attacked as Mrs. Potts had exclaimed and it was a full blown war between the Villagers and the servants aka inanimate objects.

Lumière ducked as a lady swung a pan at him, and he swiftly jumped when she tried to hit him again with it. He quickly jumped on her and her eyes followed his movements and she tried to balance herself as Lumière took a hold of her and twirled her around. He let go of her and she collapsed onto another man, who lost his balance and they both fell to the ground.

Lumière climbed the cupboard as no one was attacking him for a moment and he looked around the foyer. The foyer had turned into a war field as all the furniture around was broken or torn off to fight off the Villagers.

Lumière's eyes fell upon Chip who was in the centre of the foyer standing on a stack of saucers as he hit the Villagers with it and jumped up and down as he exclaimed, "There you go, fellas." Lumière smiled at the child as he was too innocent for his own good. His aim was good as the saucers hit the Villagers perfectly and they clenched their arms as they tried to fight off others.

Maestro Cadanza was fighting the two daughters of Lady Tremaine and Lumière laughed as he saw Maestro Cadanza dodge one of the girl's punches. He was quite swift even for his old age. He saw as Maestro Cadanza stood on his two legs and pushed the girls hard. They fell down with a thud and cursed out loud as Maestro Cadanza now stood in front of them, daring them to try. The girls looked at their mother who was now looking at them with her face scrunched, "Mama, help us!" Lady Tremaine smirked at them as she moved forward with the rifle in her hand, "Sorry, girls. It's Villain time." The girls looked at their mother's retreating form and their jaws hung in air as they couldn't believe their mother would do something like this.

"Ouch." Maestro Cadanza said as he walked away from them and rushed quickly towards Froufrou, saving him in time from getting stabbed. Maestro Cadanza hugged him as he caressed him and moved aside in time to save them from a man coming at them with an axe. Maestro Cadanza grew angry as he gathered his strength and hit the man so hard with his leg, that he flew halfway across the foyer and hit the wall, sliding down. Maestro Cadanza turned towards Froufrou and confronted him as he asked, "Are you okay, Froufrou?" Froufrou just licked his leg as he snuggled against him.

Lumière was startled as he heard Mrs. Potts shout, "How do you like your tea?" She was hanging from the huge chandelier in the middle of the foyer and she poured hot tea all over the Villagers as they grimaced loudly at the hotness, "Hot enough?" She asked as she snickered at their running forms around the foyer. Suddenly, she lost her grip on and she came falling down but, as she was about to hit the ground, Chapeau swopped her in his arms and Lumière let out a breath of relief.

He heard voices coming from the balcony. He turned towards it to find Mr. Cogsworth and Madame de Garderobe standing there with a table full of books. Mr. Cogsworth exclaimed as he looked at the books, "Ahh, yes. The inventory has arrived." He touched them and spoke, "Go teach them a lesson!" The books flew in the air at his commands and started hitting the people in the faces and Mr. Cogsworth laughed at them, "Yes, those are called books, you dimwits."

Lumière jumped as one man swung the axe at him and he jumped onto his bald head as he hit him in the head with his legs. Mr. Cogsworth took a step back as he realised that three young men were walking towards him in an angry stance. He shuddered as he spoke, "I'm just a clock." He tried reasoning as he stepped back running away from them. But, Madame Garderobe stopped as she stepped in front of them and stood with her arms on her waist, "Ahh, lovely boys!" She sang as various clothes sprung out from her drawers and the men's eyes widened as the clothes enveloped them whole and as they twirled around as Madame Garderobe dressed them in lovely gowns.

As Madame Garderobe finished, she exclaimed, "Such pretty little boys!" The men looked down at their attire and screamed as they ran off towards the main door in hurry.

Lumière's eyes searched for Plumette in the room and he chuckled as he saw her throwing dust onto the girls and laughing at their expense. Lumière resumed his attention back to spreading the fireworks around the foyer as he knew she could handle them herself.

Maestro Cadanza took a step back as he analysed the next move of the lady holding an axe in front of him. But, his attention was broken as he heard his lovely wife, Madame Garderobe exclaim as she saw him, "Maestro!" Maestro Cadanza looked up at her and smiled in delight as he said, "My love!" His gaze was fixed on her as he didn't realise that the lady in front of him was about to hit him with the axe. But, he was saved as Madame Garderobe announced, "I'm coming, my love!" Before she jumped down from the balcony onto the foyer and sent the lady in front of him flying to the table.

Lumière lit up the fireworks from the fireplace and all the Villagers went tumbling as they jumped up and down, trying to save themselves from the burn. Lumière jumped from tables to table as he sang, "It's a firework kind of night, fellas." He chuckled as he stopped next to Mr. Cogsworth. All the Villagers rushed towards the main door as they feared for their lives. Mr.

Cogsworth exclaimed as he pointed his fingers at them, "Yes! Run for your life. Out from the castle." He narrowed his eyes as he continues, "Don't come back here." Lumière chuckled at him as he folded his hands but, his eyes widened as he saw Ella walk into the foyer. She smiled lightly as she rushed towards the west wing. No one dared to stop her. They all walked outside as they saw the Villagers run towards the main entrance.

~~~

Moment de vérité - III

Third POV

Lady Tremaine smirked as she reached the bedroom of the Beast. She opened the door as she entered and looked around to find it empty. Her gaze fell upon the golds and the antiques around the room and her eyes glazed like greediness as she mentally calculated the wealth and luxury she'd get after she'd kill the Beast. She cackled in the greediness and walked further into the room. The room was dead silent and it grew colder as she walked towards the balcony slowly, not giving away her presence.

She held the rifle close to herself as she was ready to shoot the Beast if he attacked her. She reached the balcony and slowly entered it as she saw a glimpse of the Beast, crouched down on the balcony floor holding something in his hands.

She tried looking at what he held in his hands, but she was unsuccessful. So, she cleared her throat before she spoke, "Hello, Beast." The Beast turned abruptly as he was startled by her voice and looked at him. Lady Tremaine took a step back as she feared his mighty height and his fangs. He was much bigger in person and could easily kill her if he wanted to. But, at the moment he looked vulnerable so, Lady Tremaine decided to use it for her advantage.

"Ella sent me." She said as she held the rifle in front of her, pointing at him. The Beast expressions changed from vulnerable to attention at the mention of Ella's name. "She sent me to kill you." Lady Tremaine said as she smirked at him. The rifle ready to shoot if he made a move against her.

The Beast looked at her with little hope in his eyes as she continued, "Did you honestly think she'd love you?" Lady Tremaine said as she walked towards him with as much daring she could muster. The hopefulness from the Beast's eyes drained as he uttered, "She's not coming back."

Lady Tremaine's eyes were fixated on the glass slipper he held in his eyes and her eyes sparkled at them as the slippers shined brightly under the moon's light. The greediness took over her mind as she clicked the rifle in her hand and said, "She only loves her family. Not some Beast." As she finished saying this, she shot the bullet but, the bullet didn't hit the Beast and the Beast fell down along with Ella who had come to the rescue. Ella had managed to push him out of the way just in time.

The glass slipper fell from his hand onto the balcony floor and Lady Tremaine rushed quickly to catch it before it could break. She heaved out a breath as she caught it in time. She stood up as she looked at Ella who looked flustered. Lady Tremaine looked at her in confusion as she clenched the glass slippers to her chest.

Ella calmed herself as she looked at Beast and helped him up. She was flustered as she stared at his face. His expression were a mixture of every emotion and Ella couldn't place her finger on his feelings. He didn't blink as he touched her cheeks with his claws. He smiled at her as mumbled slowly, "You came back." Ella nodded at him as she blushed, "I tried stopping them." She said as she touched his forearm.

The little moment was broken as they heard another gun shot. They ducked as they tried to protect themselves. But, they didn't get hurt as the bullet wasn't aimed for them and it was fired in the air. They looked at Lady Tremaine in disbelief as she cackled to herself absentmindedly. She cocked the rifle to her side as she uttered, scoffing, "So, now what, huh? The Princess gets to live happily ever after with the Prince? Huh?" She walked around the balcony as she looked down.

"Madam-" Ella started as she walked towards her but, she stopped in her tracks as her stepmother lifted her gaze and looked at Ella. Ella took a step back as she feared the hatred and ugliness that filled her stepmother's eyes.

"Don't! Don't use that voice on me." She scrunched her face in annoyance as she said, "I despise your voice. Didn't you understand that yet?" She let out a laugh as she looked at Ella's confused face, "You use the sweet, innocent voice on everyone and they just melt at your innocence. They fall at your feet as they worship your kindness." Ella tries not to fazed by her words as she steps towards her in order to stop her. The Beast followed her movements as he too carefully stepped towards her.

"Don't you come near me." Lady Tremaine warned them as she shook her head, tears spilling. She looked frantic as she kept on shaking her head as she tightly clenched the slippers to her chest. "I was like you once, you see. But, than one day I met your mother and.. and I hated her because she was so perfect." Lady Tremaine knocked her head with the rifle as she recalled her younger self.

"She just was so perfect and..and.. I....I tried to be like her, you know. But," She stopped looking at the ground as she looked at the Beast, "But, I couldn't be her. Instead, I became like him." She pointed the rifle in the Beast's direction. Ella gasped as she tried making sense of the happenings. The Beast looked at her in confusion as she smiled evilly at them. "I became ugly and selfish like him." This angered the Beast. "I became the Beast!" She roared out loud as she laughed like a crazy maniac.

The Beast stomped angrily towards her and Lady Tremaine gasped out loud as he picked her up with his right hand and choked her. He held her high in the air and she was dangling from the balcony. Lady Tremaine chocked as she tried speaking, "Please, don't let go of me." She struggled for words as she continued, "Beast...Please,...I'll do anything." The Beast narrowed his eyes as he placed her back on the floor, still in a choke hold as he muttered, loud and clear, "I'm not a Beast." He scoffed as he released her from his grip and pushed her away. She struggled to breath as she coughed out, trying to calm her breathing. He turned to see Ella standing wide eyed as dumbfounded.

"Ella," He began as he walked towards her slowly, her eyes turned towards him and he sighed in relief as the life returned to her eyes, "I'm so sorry." She shook her head at him as he reached her and took his hand in hers as she focused her attention on him.

He adored her as she caressed his hands, eyes full of tears. She chuckled lightly at him. Her gaze landed behind him and her eyes widened as she saw her stepmother reading to shoot the bullet. Ella exclaimed, "No!" as she quickly turned him around and gasped as the bullet hit her in the back. The Beast's eyes widened as he looked at the stepmother. As he caught Ella in his arms, another gun shot was heard as the stepmother loaded the rifle.

The second last rose petal fell as the castle shook. The balcony Ella's stepmother was standing on collapsed as Lady Tremaine shot another bullet at Ella and it hit her in the shoulders. The balcony fell down as it took Lady Tremaine along with the glass slipper in her hand and she yelled as she fell to death.

The Beast's eyes teared as he looked at Ella. She was bleeding frantically as he quickly picked her up and walked inside. He placed her on the floor as she stared at him sadly. He lost his senses as he stared at the blood ruining her dress. He was reminded of his mother's death and he shook his head as he focused on her. He pressed down on the wound as Ella winced at his claw but, he had to do it to stop the blood flood.

The Beast looked at his bedroom as he yelled, "Lumière! Cogsworth! Mrs. Potts!" He tried to call them but, to no avail. "Anyone? Help us here." He yelled as he waited for a response but was met with silence. Ella smiled sadly at him as she touched his cheek with her palm, "It's okay. It's okay." She murmured as caressed his cheek. He shook with the sobs as he looked at her. "At least, I get to see you for the last time." She said as she clenched his palm in hers and squeezed for reassurance. "Promise me one thing." She began as she crocked through the pain, "Take care of my father. Please look after him." He nodded vigorously at her request and kissed her forehead as he said, "I promise. Promise. Please, don't leave me Ella." He hugged her as he sobbed heavily.

The Enchantress walked into his bedroom and removed her cloak as she stared at the pair lying on the floor. Her gaze fell upon the rose, the last petal dangling onto the edge. Her eyes followed the pair and she saw as Ella spoke, "I want you to be happy." The Beast nodded at her as he couldn't comprehend her words and wanted to save her at all cost.

"I love you." Ella said as another tear escaped her eyes and she smiled at him lightly as the last petal fell and her eyes closed. The Beast's eyes widened as her eyes closed and he couldn't believe as he shook her dead body, trying to wake her up. He looked around helplessly as he held her still body. He laid his ear to her chest as he tried to check her heart beat. Her body's temperature dropped quickly as all the warmth left her body and he shivered from the cold.

He violently shook her body as he couldn't believe his eyes. He sobbed as he sat down and held her body in his arms. He hugged tightly as he closed his eyes not wanting to see the reality. "You have to come back."

The Enchantress smiled as she touched the glass covering the rose, and it broke into million pieces as she waved her hands around the petals and all the petals formed the rose, leaving one back. Half of the rose petals flew towards the Beast. The rose petals covered him like a second skin and the golden hue surrounded him. The Beast was engaged in sobbing as he didn't realise that he had turned back into a human being. He rocked back and forth as he hugged her close to himself.

His eyes widened as he heard footsteps and looked up to find the Enchantress standing in front of him. He looked down at his hands and gasped as he took in the reality. The Enchantress bent down as she placed the rose on Ella's chest and she turned towards him as she said, "She died for you."

Prince Adam roared out loud, "No!" as the Enchantress vanished into thin air and the castle came back to life.

~~~

fin.

www.ingramcontent.com/pod-product-compliance
Lightning Source LLC
Chambersburg PA
CBHW072157070526
44585CB00015B/1190